AMAZING LOVE, IT CAN BE
A Memoir

Robert Magarian

Cover design: Peter O'Connor
www.bespokebookcovers.com

Interior photos courtesy of the author's personal collection.
Author (Magarian) Photo: "shevyvision"
Shevaun Williams & Associates, Norman, OK
www.shevaunwilliams.com

Editing: Nancy Hancock

Print formatting: Bravia Books, LLC

ISBN (Print): 979-8-9914614-0-5

Contents

ALSO BY ROBERT MAGARIAN

Fiction
The Watchman
72 Hours
You'll Never See Me Again, A Crime to Remember
The Tongue Collector
Forever Young

Nonfiction
Amazing Love, It Can Be
A Memoir

Essays
Follow Your Dream
A Journey into Faith

DEDICATION

This book is dedicated to those persons thinking about giving their lives to another in marriage. The vision of uniting with another person seems surreal, but soon you'll learn that the act of giving oneself to another is saintly—a bond that involves feelings of deep affection and tenderness filled with God's grace.

IN MARRIAGE WE MUST BELIEVE

As for husbands, love your wives just like Christ loved the church and gave himself for her.

—Ephesians 5:25 (Life Application Bible NIV)

Love is patient. Love is kind. it does not envy, it does not boast, it is not proud. It is not rude, it is not self-seeking, it is not easily angered, it keeps no record of wrongs. Love does not delight in evil but rejoices with the truth. It always protects, always trusts, always hopes, always pervers.

—1 Corinthians 13:4-7 (Life Application Bible NIV)

…a man will leave his father and mother and be united to his wife, and they will become one flesh.

—Genesis 2:24 (Life Application Bible NIV)

AMAZING LOVE

This is our story, this is our song,
Enduring love carried us along.
A voice from above, come follow me,
Miracles happen when you do;
Spirit and power comes alive within you.
Amazing love, what is the key,
The love of God living in me.
So much you'll discover;
Sacrificing for another.
One and only love,
Comes from above.
We give our life to you,
In all we say and all we do.
Amazing love supported us through,
The best of times, the worst of times;
The Lord's hand touched our hearts,
Cleared our minds.
Amazing love is true,
Not meant for just a few.
We survived so long,
Many years and going strong.

—Robert Magarian

INTRODUCTION

This is a story about Bob Magarian and Charmaine Magarian, who grew up during the depression of the thirties and forties, met, fell in love, married, and shared a loving life together. which is illustrated in the events of their seventy-seven years from the time they met (1947) to the present (2024). These were the best of times, the worst of times.

Much detail is provided in this work so the reader can sense the impact of their love for one another as they survived life's tribulations.

While it wasn't the original intent for their story to evolve into a family chronicle—which hopefully is a "magnum opus" in reporting and memory—heartwarming, curious, sometimes funny and sometimes sad—but it couldn't be avoided.

The questions asked most often of the couple: How did you survive all those years together? What is your secret? Your story?

Early in their marriage, Bob and Charmaine experienced a sense of God's presence, whom they believe directed their lives. Scripture taught them how to act toward one another, like Jesus loved and sacrificed himself for his church. In like manner, they felt and understood as husband and wife the love and the need of sacrifice for one another.

In this story, it is hoped the reader will recognize the keynotes in the storyline: (1) *Effective living is not measured as much by what they accomplished, as by what they overcame to accomplish it; (2) Those who are obedient grow in understanding, (3) Love is more powerful than time, wealth, or wisdom that is accessible in this world, and (4) Anything of significance is accomplished in relationship with God.*

CHAPTER 1
When It All Started

Little did I know that my life was about to change on this beautiful, sunny autumn morning in late September of 1947. I stepped out of the city bus at the corner stop, close to East Side High in East St. Louis, Illinois. I was a senior, looking forward to my June graduation so I could get on with my life and enter college. The thought of college thrilled me, but high school, while necessary, didn't do much for me. It wasn't that I was arrogant, it's just that I wanted to move on to help people. My father was a physician and after working intermittently with him for four years, I had this yearning to go to med school.

I entered the northside doors of the East Side High School building and moseyed to my locker to hang up my jacket and retrieve a few items for class, then sat in my home room waiting for the bell to ring, announcing time to begin the school day. A few minutes later, it rang, and I walked down the hall through a crowd of students for my first class, American History, and entered the classroom on my left. Our teacher, a tall, lanky, pleasant man with gray hair and narrow face, appeared to be in his early sixties. I really liked his personality and his teaching, I'm sorry that I don't remember his name. The first two rows from the door were unoccupied but the other four rows were filled. I sat in the last desk in the second row, the fourth row from the door.

I don't know what came over me this day, but after sitting at the same desk for nearly two weeks, I felt this strange urge to move to the front. I didn't have a difficult time hearing our teacher, and it surprised me that I stood up before the class started and asked if I could move to the front. He was kind and told me to sit wherever I wished. As I walked up the second row from the door, I stopped at the front empty desk and looked to my left at a beautiful, smiling, round-faced girl. I jokingly told the teacher, "I'll sit next to this girl. She looks smart." She smiled at me again.

At the next class meeting, I asked pretty-face what her name was. I learned it was Charmaine Kugler. She asked me mine. Just looking at her, I got a feeling something was pulling me to her. After a few classes, we began talking more and I found her very pleasant, the kind of girl I liked. She had a glow about her, seemed shy, but not afraid to talk.

The next morning while I was seated in the Rosemont bus that went by our high school, the driver stopped at the corner of Lynch and Eighteenth Street, about a mile from my home. I was seated in the middle of the bus and as I looked out the window, I saw Charmaine waiting at the bus stop with a man who could be her dad. She boarded the bus and walked down the aisle towards me. She was wearing a head scarf wrapped around her pretty face. My heart began to race. As she approached me and smiled, I heard this still small voice say, "*She is going to be your wife.*"

The voice reminded me of the spiritual experience I had once when I was thirteen years old, playing basketball with friends in the courtyard of Holy Angels Church on Caseyville Avenue, about a mile east of my home. As I came down from laying up the ball at the basket, I felt in the blink of an eye, something like a sun ray shoot into my head and flow down to my feet. I looked around, puzzled. None of my friends said anything.

What in the world just happened to me, I thought.

I never told my parents nor anyone else about it, and in a few days, I forgot about it, until now. When Charmaine walked by me, I knew I had to make my *way* to the back exit before she got off at the school bus stop.

When the driver stopped at our school stop, I hurried to the back in time to get off behind her. She smiled at me, and I said, "Hi." What else could I say. She smiled and said, "Hi."

"Can I walk you to class?" I said, flustered. There was no need to ask. We both were going in that direction, but I didn't know what else to say.

She said, "Sure."

I asked if she lived closed to the bus stop where she boarded the bus. She said she lived on Natalie Ave, a couple of blocks north of the bus stop. I told her I lived on Caseyville Ave, across from Jones Park. As we walked along, I learned she just had a birthday on the 15th, ten days earlier. Turned sixteen. I mentioned I turned seventeen earlier in July. When we entered the school building, she went to her home room and I went to mine after saying, "I'll see you in class." We continued to talk before class and after class, but I didn't have the nerve to ask her out for a date just yet.

A few classes later she brought a picture of herself taken at Olin Mills and showed it to me. In the picture she was wearing a checkered dress.

Such a pretty thing, I thought, as I held it in my hand.

I was hoping she wanted me to keep it; otherwise, why would she show it to me? I wanted to ask for it but didn't know if I should. I finally got the nerve to ask, and she said I could have it. *Did that mean she liked me? I wondered. I hoped.*

I wanted to ask her out for a date but chickened out again. Instead, she asked if I ever went dancing at the St. Paul's Center. It was a building connected to St. Paul's Episcopal Church that was across the street from Rock Junior High, adjacent to our high school. She said most of the students went dancing there every Friday night. I had never been. We sorta made a date for the coming Friday night, when I said I would see her there. That meant I had four days to get up the nerve to go. I got my brother Leon to go with me. When we entered the Center, I saw Charmaine dancing with her girlfriend Erna. In those days, girls danced together. When Charmaine spotted me coming in, she hurried over to greet me, smiling. Her girlfriend, Erna, came with her and paired up with Leon.

Charmaine, a five-foot- two brunette with a sweet smile that emphasized her blue eyes, was wearing a blue plaid skirt and a blue sweater. She was the first girl I ever danced with, and it felt good

3

holding her against me. I wasn't a good dancer, but I knew then I'd never let her go. I'll never forget the popular cologne she was wearing, *Heaven Scent*. I thought, *what an appropriate name*, I had this feeling, the Lord was bringing us together. *A match made in Heaven. Was that what the voice meant when it said she was mine?*

We spent the evening together with Leon and Erna and left around ten o'clock and took the girls home. I now knew where Charmaine lived, which was a little over a mile or so from my home. I walked her to the door and hesitated. I wanted to kiss her, but I just told her how I enjoyed being with her and hoped we could do it again. She smiled and nodded.

CHAPTER 2
Getting To Know One Another

A week later, on a Saturday afternoon, I was working outside our home with my dad and several Armenian men, fixing our basement windows. To my amazement and joy, here came Charmaine with one of her girlfriends. I introduced her to my dad. The Armenian men, standing around were smiling at me. I never saw my dad, who we called Hydig (Our variation as kids of *hayrik* for father in Armenian), so pleased to see someone. I didn't know if he thought I finally got a girlfriend or what he was thinking. He never said. But I was pleased how he acted toward her. I then took Charmaine and her girlfriend inside to meet my mother. She, too, was happy to meet Charmaine. They hit it off right away. I felt like I was king for the day. Later, Charmaine told me she didn't know why she did such a thing, coming to my house.

I thought I did. *Maybe she was beginning to like me.*

After that we went on two Saturday evening dates to the movies in St. Louis, either to the Lowe's theatre or the Ambassador theatre. East St. Louis was connected to St. Louis with several bridges over the Mississippi river. It was like going downtown to go to St. Louis. The Lowe's was on the main street, Washington Boulevard, not far from the bus depot, and the Ambassador was on a side street close by. Since I didn't have a car, we had to go by bus, After the movie we had dessert in one of the ice cream shops before boarding the last

Rosemount bus to the Illinois side—the one that stopped two blocks from Charmaine's home. During our first real date, I walked her to her house thinking, *tonight I'm going to plant my first kiss*.

How was I going to do it?

Just do it, I thought. *Become a man!*

Charmaine held my arm as we walked the two blocks from the bus stop in the dim light from only one streetlight a block away. She looked pretty in her brown overcoat, and the smell of her cologne was getting to me. When we reached the porch, the light was on. She turned to say something but before she got a word out, I planted my first two-second kiss. She smiled and then went in. I was pleased with myself as I began retracing the two blocks and turning on Lynch Avenue for the mile-long walk home in the dark. It was midnight.

It was scary. Too quiet. No cars.

There was only one streetlight between two railroad crossings separated by two blocks. A gateman (watchman) at the second railroad crossing was twenty feet up in his enclosed watchtower, which looked like a little house. Automatic gates were unheard of during that time. They were manually lowered by a watchman. Someone had to operate the gates from inside the factory office at the first crossing, because there was no watchtower. The gateman at the second crossing always waved at me, which felt good. Someone was watching me, I had hoped.

I must really be in love to walk this mile, I thought, as I trekked in the dark waiting for someone or some animal to jump out at me. I made it home feeling relieved and unscathed.

After several dates, I was becoming more attached to Charmaine, but wasn't sure how she felt about me, or if she thought I was the one for her. Yes, after each date, I continued walking that mile home in the moonlight. True love.

In early November, I went to Chicago by train with my brother Leon and several other students for a weekend session involving a school project, which began on Friday morning and ending Saturday afternoon. While in Chicago, I couldn't get Charmaine out of my mind, and during a break in the program I went to a jewelry store and bought her a brooch. I had planned to give it to her when we'd get together Sunday evening. Leon and I arrived home late Sunday afternoon. I called Charmaine from our landline phone and was surprised that she was so pleased to hear from me, a reaction I hadn't witnessed before. This time I asked my folks if I could use the family car to pick her up.

That first time when she visited our home and met my dad and mom was a smart move on her part, because now my folks knew I was going with her, and when I asked to use the car, they'd first ask if it was with Charmaine. Of course it was she. I never dated anyone else. Knowing it was Charmaine made it okay.

When I drove up to her house, she was waiting for me on the porch and hurried to my car. I noticed a change in her once she got in and sat close to me. She was livelier and bubbly. She told me how much she missed me. I, in turn, told her how I thought about her the whole time I was in Chicago. I didn't talk about the trip. We went to one of the drive-ins for some refreshments and I had a hard time not giving her the broach. When I took her home and parked in front of her house, I told her I had a present for her, and reached into my jacket pocket and handed her the box. She quickly opened it and was so surprised and thankful. She took it out of the box and asked me to pin it on her. Then we sat for a while talking about our feelings. She surprised me with what she told her mother while I was gone that, "Bob was the one for me." I told her I felt the same about her and wanted us to go steady. She agreed. After a couple of five-second kisses, I walked her up to the porch. I now knew in my heart we would be getting married someday.

*Haig and Anahid behind
Bob & Charmaine*

CHAPTER 3
Meeting Charmaine's Parents

This Friday night in November, Charmaine had made plans for me to meet her parents, Joe and Marie Kugler. She had been telling her mother and grandmother Roy and great grandmother Carrie about me and I knew someday we would all be meeting. But tonight was just with her parents. All day I thought about how they would receive me. I finally told myself,

"Stop worrying, you'll soon find out."

I left home around six-thirty and Charmaine met me at the door, smiled and ushered me in. Marie Kugler, an attractive, slender brunette in her mid-thirties with a pleasant smile and attractive narrow face, was wearing a wool blouse and skirt, stood up from the couch to greet me. Charmaine said, "This is Bob Magarian." I felt the warmth in her eyes and demeanor, which I accepted as approval. Seconds later, a bald, round-faced man with a slender body, in his late thirties, came out of a bedroom to the left of the door, wearing a long—sleeved blue shirt and khaki pants, eyeing me with a frown. He had to be a 32" waist, looked strong and healthy. He wasn't smiling. Charmaine introduced me. We shook hands and then Charmaine waved for me to sit next to her on the couch. Marie was seated next to her daughter. The living room was large enough for a couch and two overstuffed chairs. A coal furnace positioned midway against the wall was giving off heat. Another bedroom opened from the living room a few feet from where

I was sitting. I could see into the kitchen. I didn't feel the warmth from Charmaine's dad that I did from her mother. Joe Kugler sat in a chair in the corner of the room and began asking me about my parents and my siblings. That was my gambit to talk about my family history. He seemed to mellow after I had finished. While he didn't ask me, I thought I'd tell him my goal, so he didn't think I was a loser. I told him my plan was to go to medical school, following my dad's footsteps. He just smiled but said nothing.

Charmaine was observing me the entire time. Joe told me how he worked on the docks of Nickle Plate Railroad loading and unloading merchandise. No wonder he was in good shape. Marie didn't say much, smiled a lot. I felt she had accepted me. We had some coffee and cake and then Charmaine and I left. Outside, I asked if she thought her dad trusted me. She thought he did.

I learned a week later that Chamaine's dad talked to one of his coworkers, an Armenian man who happened to be a friend of our family, but Joe didn't know it. Joe knew Nishan, being Armenian, would know the Magarians, and he asked about me. Later, I learned from Nishan that he told Joe there were no finer boys than the Magarian boys and the family was highly respected. After that, Charmaine's dad seemed friendlier towards me and now took more interest in what I was planning on doing with my life. College was the topic. I never said, "I am going to marry your daughter," but I felt like it. After our talk, we spent weekends watching wrestling matches on a little TV screen, in one of the first TVs that came out in 1947. The screen was extremely small—six inches in width and about five inches in height.

CHAPTER 4
High School Graduation and College

I graduated from East Side High in June 1948. That summer I worked at the Aluminum Ore Company as a laborer and made six hundred dollars, which was a good sum back then. I used some of the money towards tuition at Belleville Junior College. I really wanted to attend Washington University in St. Louis, a very prestigious university, but couldn't afford the tuition. A semester cost $350. In contrast, if I went to the University of Illinois up north in Champaign, I would pay only $19.00 per semester as a resident. Hence, Washington U was 18 times more expensive. I could have asked my dad for tuition money but because I wanted to go it alone, I didn't. I knew he would have helped if I had asked, but he taught me to be self-sufficient, and besides, I was hoping he'd offer without my asking, but he didn't.

That fall, not having a car, I was compelled to ride the city bus downtown and transfer to the Belleville bus line for the 29-mile trip into the city, whose city limit was adjacent to East St. Louis. The College was in behind the high school that was close to downtown. The classrooms and student union were in barracks. I wasn't impressed with the place and found it depressing. The teacher quality was just a little above high-school level, and their methods were not very good. My sight was set on Washington University.

I had a teacher in English literature at the Junior College who didn't like me or my writing style. Every essay that I had written, she gave me a C- grade. One day in one of the side rooms in my dad's office, I was frustrated while working on my next essay. I had outlined and wrote a short synopsis to see where I was going. The dentist that had his office and examining rooms across from my dad's, stepped in and asked what I was doing. I explained what I had been facing with my English teacher, and that I thought she didn't like me and/or my writing. He suggested that he would be glad to help me. He had attended the University of Illinois and got all A's in his essays. He looked over what I had written and suggested that he could write my essay as an experiment to test my theory about the teacher. I suggested that that would be like plagiarizing and I didn't know if I wanted to do that. To make me feel better he waited until I had finished writing my essay and then he revised what I wrote. In all honesty, he had essentially written my essay. "Now let's see what grade you get," he said. "It should be and A."

I turned in my essay and waited in anticipation. Several days later I saw the stack of papers on her desk. I had a hard time concentrating, waiting for her to pass out our papers at the end of the class. When the bell rang, she began passing them out as we were leaving. When she handed mine, she didn't look at me. I looked at the grade as I left the room. There was a big C in the right corner of my paper. No C- this time, but a C.

I was eager to take my paper to my dad's office to show Dr. L. my grade. He exploded. "She has it in for you! I need to talk to her!" I waited until he calmed down and told him let's forget it. There's not anything I can do about it.

During Christmas, 1948, Charmaine joined our family gathering. I remember well Charmaine's first present she gave me—a carton of Lucky Strike cigarettes and a Zippo lighter. At that time, a Zippo lighter was the best of lighters and the most-sold lighter. Oh, yes, smoking was the thing back then.

Charmaine was graduated from East Side High in January 1949 and went to work in the billing office of Swift Packing Company in the Stock Yards. In June 1949, I completed one year of pre-med at Belleville Jr. College, and was ready to move on but couldn't. I was lucky that year to make friends with the Baldwin twins, who owned a car and offered to pick me up and bring me home if I shared in the gas, which I was happy to do. We became good friends, and I owed them a lot, since I no longer had to ride the bus.

I got my second summer job working in the factory of East Louis Casting on the 4 pm to 12 midnight shift. My job was to make sure the journeymen's sand boxes were full of sand so they could continue to make patterns for different auto, appliance, and hardware parts. There was much competition between the journeymen, since they were paid by the piece and not on hourly salary. Consequently, one of them would always be on my tail about filling his sand box before the other guys. I found him obnoxious.

When I wasn't filling sand boxes, I worked the oven where the sand patterns came down a conveyor belt. I reached for them and placed them on the rotating oven racks so the sand would "cook." I made good money but was glad when the summer job was over.

In late fall of 1949, I was back in Belleville Junior College and felt it was time to ask Charmaine to marry me or I was going to flunk out of school. I couldn't keep coming over to see her when I needed to study. But I was weak and had to see her on weekends. I wasn't planning on us marrying right away, but in about a year. It was time to make my move.

CHAPTER 5
Our Engagement

In November of 1949, I purchased a set of engagement and wedding rings with some financial help from my sweet mother. I had to save for tuition and ancillary expenses, so I was pleased mom said she'd like to help me.

This Friday evening around seven-thirty, I borrowed the family car with my mother's approval. She smiled knowing what I was up to. When I met Charmaine at her home for our date, I told her we only had time to go for a hamburger and coke because I had a big test in Zoo coming up and couldn't stay too long. She was always supportive and understanding. She didn't suspect anything. On our way back to her house, I was running my proposal through my mind. I couldn't wait to get parked in front of her house to propose to her and slip the ring on her finger.

My heart was racing.

Once I parked, I had to say something to distract her from seeing me reaching into my left jacket pocket for the ring. I told her we needed to think about getting married or I was going to flunk out of school, spending so much time away from my studies. "I'll never get into med school if I don't keep my grades up," I emphasized. I only had the engagement ring in its box. There was no problem flipping it open in my pocket while we were talking. It was dark and she didn't notice I had the ring in my hand.

I reached for her hand like I was going to squeeze it, and quickly slipped the ring on her ring finger, and said, "Charmaine, you know I love you and want to marry you—"

—She screamed. The passenger side door flew open. She darted out without allowing me to finish my proposal and rushed into the house. I quickly shot after her, disappointed that I didn't finish my proposal. When I entered the open door, she was in the kitchen showing the ring to her mother. Her mother smiled at me and then hugged me. Her dad came through the kitchen wondering what all the commotion was. He smiled and congratulated us. Thank God he was pleased. He wasn't one to show his emotions. We ended up celebrating with ice cream, cake, and coffee.

After our unexpected celebration, I asked Charmaine to step out on the porch. I wanted to talk. I told her it was now time for us to plan our wedding. She agreed. This I was glad to hear because once we had this discussion about or future and she said she wanted to try and help her mother a little financially. But now, I told Charmaine that her mother had been making her way and it was now time to think about our future. I could see where she was coming from because ever since Charmaine was a teenager she had to work odd jobs to buy her clothes, shoes, and everything for her bedroom—bed sheets, pillowcases and blankets. At fifteen, she went to work at a bag company in St. Louis during the summer, where she cut the bags to separate them as they came out of the large sewing machines. She made $31 per week and her dad made her give $10 to her mother. During the school year, Charmaine worked weekends and summers at S.S. Kresge's department store downtown in East St. Louis until she graduated from high school.

CHAPTER 6
Our Wedding and Reception

During the planning of our wedding, we had to consider not having much money. Charmaine's folks couldn't pay for the wedding, so, we prudently planned within our means. We chose to go to Branson, Missouri for our honeymoon, and spend the first night in a hotel in St. Louis. Our reception would be held in my parents' home in our decorated basement. It was no ordinary basement. It had tiled walls and was very livable. We spent a couple of days decorating and preparing food and drinks, setting up the chairs and tables, and Mom had a beautiful wedding cake on order. My father was nice enough to offer his red Oldsmobile for us to use on our honeymoon.

The day I had been waiting for since I met Charmaine had arrived—Saturday, June 24, 1950. I remember it well. After Leon, my best man, and I showered in late afternoon, we laid on our twin beds looking up at the ceiling, wondering how the day was all going to turn out. I felt a little apprehensive. Not about getting married, but how the wedding and all would go; especially the reception, since we weren't having it in any banquet hall. Charmaine and I had met with Pastor Talley at the Methodist Church, and our pre-marital session went well.

Charmaine had purchased her wedding dress material and a neighbor, who lived a block away, made her dress. She was noted for being the best seamstress around. The service was to start at seven p.m. We were told to arrive at 6:15 p.m.

It was time to get dressed in our rented tuxedos. I looked in the mirror when finished and whispered, "Not bad, you good-looking devil." Of course, I was trying to be funny to quiet my nerves.

Leon said, "That'll be the day."

We laughed. Didn't know he heard me.

Leon drove me to the church in the red Olds I was going to use on our honeymoon. When we arrived, the parking lot was half-full. We parked and entered the church from the side entrance, where we met up with Pastor Talley, who smiled and asked how I felt.

"I believe I'll survive, sir," I said, followed by a big smile.

"You'll be fine," he said. "Just relax for now."

We went into the room next to his office.

I walked around the room, wondering what Charmaine was doing. Of course we hadn't spoken since the night before. I guessed, she and Erna, her maid of honor, were getting her ready for our big event.

Reverend Tally poked his head in the room and asked, "Are you ready?"

"I guess," I said.

"You'll be fine, Robert," he said. "Just think about that beautiful bride you'll be united with soon."

I was trying.

We followed him through the side door that led into the sanctuary.

As practiced, we moved to one side facing the audience, with Leon behind me. Reverend Tally stood in the middle looking down the aisle.

The organist began playing. I didn't know what. I was concentrating on the friends and family being ushered into the church.

I looked around and saw my mother and father and all our family in the front row and my uncle's family behind them. My mother looked like she was at my funeral, wiping her eyes and had a sad look. My father was smiling. I knew what he was thinking:

I'm not losing a son, I'm gaining a daughter.

As the organist played her last piece before the Wedding March, Erna, the maid of honor, wearing a pink Sleeveless Lace Bridesmaid Dress, slowly made her way down the aisle toward us carrying a bouquet of beautiful flowers, and as she approached the steps, she moved over to one side, smiling.

My mother who finally realized she wasn't at my funeral but at my wedding; for now, she was looking at me and smiling. I winked at her to convey, "All is going to be fine, mom. I'm alive and well."

Suddenly, I saw a figure wearing the prettiest white wedding dress ever move into view in the back, turning, facing the front holding her father's arm. I couldn't see Charmaine's face, but the dress was magnificent.

This is the greatest day of my life, I thought with my heart racing.

Then the organist began the Wedding March, and everyone stood up and faced the back as Charmaine and her father proceeded slowly down the aisle towards the front.

As they processed towards us, Charmaine with her face covered and holding beautiful flowers. I looked at her dad, who wasn't smiling. He looked scared. When they approached us, Charmaine handed her flowers to Erna and then lifted her veil.

Oh, my gosh, such a beautiful face! My heart was racing again. I was ready for the honeymoon.

Reverend Talley asked who was giving this bride away. Her dad, said, "Her mother and I." Then he turned and sat in the front pew next to his wife, Marie. Charmaine smiled at me, which melted my heart.

When is the honeymoon? I thought. *I'm only human.*

I reached for her hand and placed it into my arched arm and helped her up the two steps into the sanctuary where we faced Reverend Tally, who then told the audience to sit, and he began the service. Charmaine felt warm next to me and smelled so good. At first, I didn't hear a word Reverend Tally said. I wanted to take Charmaine in my arms and smother her with kisses.

We said our yeses to: "In the name of God, do you _____ take _____ to your wife/husband, to have and to hold from this day forward, for better, for worse, for richer, for poorer, in sickness and in health, to love and cherish until death do you part?" Leon handed me her wedding band and I placed it on her ring finger. She took my hand and slipped the wedding band she bought me down to my knuckle but couldn't push it past it. I covered her hand and pushed it on.

Reverend Tally then pronounced us Husband and Wife.

"You can kiss the bride," he said turning to me.

You bet, I will. *I'll kiss her from here to heaven.*

I grabbed her and gave her a five-second kiss.

Reverend Tally turned to the audience, and said, "Welcome, Mr. and Mrs. Robert Magarian."

Everyone clapped and the organist began playing as we marched out at a quicker pace than when she came down the aisle. After the photographer took several pictures of Charmaine and me, and then several of the wedding party, which included my Best Man, Leon, and our Maid of Honor, Erna Ashcroft, we exited the front of the church only to have rice thrown at us and a lot of cheering. It was kinda fun getting all that attention. Leon drove us around with the windows painted in white, "Just Married," and then to our home.

In June 1950, air conditioning wasn't prevalent. It wasn't until the end of the year that air conditioners appeared in homes, and not until the 1970s was Central Air Conditioning implemented in most commercial buildings. A lot of rotating fans were used in homes. Charmaine told me she slept with her head close to an open window with a fan blowing, something no one would dare do today.

The basements were the coolest places to be. So, it wasn't too out of place to have our reception there. When we entered, some of our relatives were waiting for us, to give us a few hugs and kisses. Our photographer was snapping pictures at every turn. I looked around and saw the place really looked nice with all the decorations and the way the tables and chairs were arranged. Everyone was laughing and seemed to be having an enjoyable time talking to one another. I guess I worried for nothing.

Once the wedding party was seated at the head table, family members began serving the food. The photographer was still working the place.

The huge wedding cake stood tall in front of us. While eating, I looked around and saw everyone enjoying themselves. My worries had been for nothing, except for one to come: a task I despised with a purple passion; opening presents in front of everyone. I looked to my right and on a long table were the presents. I couldn't help but wonder who started this custom of opening presents and reading off the item and names of those who gave it. It could be embarrassing for the giver.

When Charmane and I finished eating, I looked around and saw that most of our guests were done. So, it was cake time. I caught their attention by tapping my glass with a fork. I rose and started my little talk, welcoming everyone and telling them how much Charmaine and I appreciated their coming for our special day. A few flashes from the photographer almost blinded me. I signaled to my aunt that it was time to distribute the cake. Charmaine removed the top layer, and put it in the box, and gave it to her to store for our future use. Charmaine picked up the ribbon-covered knife by the cake and placed it on the next layer, waiting for me to put my hand over hers to cut out our piece. Once we did, we both held it so we could take a bite. There was enthusiastic cheering the whole time and flashes from the photographer. We sat while a couple of our relatives began distributing cake to everyone.

Even though we had circulating fans blowing in all directions and it was much cooler than the June heat outside, we were beginning to feel warm in our wedding outfits. Sweat was dripping down from under my arms and sliding down my sides. I caught Charmaine blowing the hair out of her face and saw perspiration popping up on her forehead. She whispered to me that she was beginning to feel the heat. I answered, "As soon as we open all the presents, we'll leave."

I stood up and said, "Folks, I believe one last thing Charmaine and I need to do before leaving is opening the presents." Again, they cheered.

I could tell most were waiting for this moment and turned to face us as we moved over to the side table, I whispered to Charmaine to move the wrappings and items out of the way once I opened them.

I picked up the first present, read the card, opened the box, and held up the gift, and then I thanked the person or family. I continued this process until all presents were opened. There was an embarrassing moment awaiting me. Two-pint bottles of Jack Daniels whiskey held together by ribbon and a card sitting by itself were staring at me. I knew who it was from and acted like I had overlooked it. Well, the man who gave them to us was well known by everyone as a heavy drinker and I didn't want to recognize his gift because it was alcohol.

Charmaine and I didn't drink. You guessed it. He called out. "Bob, don't forget my present." I made an excuse, held up his two bottles, gave his name and thanked him and made some remark about needing this after a long day of studying.

It was time to leave and none too soon. Charmaine's hair was a disaster, and her dress was beginning to look wrinkled. Sweat was rolling down my forehead and back. My shirt was wet, and my tux jacket was wrinkled.

Char's Parents & Bob's Parents

CHAPTER 7

Our Honeymoon

The plan was to leave the reception and head to Charmaine's folks to change out of our weeding outfits before going to the hotel in St. Louis for the night. After arriving at the Kugler's home, we went into Charmaine's old bedroom, now empty of all her personal belongings, and started removing our formal wear and putting on our regular clothes, I took my formal shirt to the sink and rang all the sweat out of it and hung it on a hanger with the tux for her father to take back to the shop downtown while we were away.

Joe and Marie came in as we were about to leave. I told him where the tux was hanging and thanked him for taking my tux back to the store. He said it was no problem. The way he looked at me was a little strange. Don't know if he wanted to congratulate me, or he was proud that I was his son-n-law, or if now he realized that his daughter would no longer be with them. We never hugged and he never said.

Charmaine paid for most of the wedding and reception with some help from me that came from my summer job. Fortunately, we paid for our honeymoon cottage earlier, and the money we received in the gifts at the reception was going to be a big help. After our first night together in the hotel, we left the next morning for Branson. On our way we had to stop for lunch and in the restaurant some men were looking at us and I felt a little jealous, not wanting anyone to look at my pretty bride. Several hours later we followed the road that ran through the town of Branson, with only two stop signs. Beyond that we'd be driving out of town.

Branson in 1950 was a one-horse town, consisting of one café, a Chevy Dealer, and sprawling acres of land and lakes. That afternoon we found Lonnie Lee Cottages about a mile from the café and checked in. We learned that the owners were originally from Chicago. Our cottage was very nice and clean and had a large swimming pool. Each cottage had its own entrance and was a one bedroom with kitchenette, bath, small living area with one couch and an overstuff chair and a side table. That afternoon we found a store to get some groceries.

The next morning after a late breakfast, I went out and sat in the cushioned chair on the small front porch in front of our cottage to enjoy the sun and to think about what had happened to me—the feeling that came over me at breakfast. Charmaine came out wearing her bathing suit and told me she was going to sit by the pool, and wondered if I were coming. I told her I'd join her in a little bit. She couldn't swim and I knew she wouldn't be going into the water without me.

I didn't mention I wanted to be alone for a while to figure out what this message was that I received. That is, if it were a message. Whatever it was, or whomever caused it, a stream of thoughts flooded my mind about what had happened between Charmaine and me the last two days. Now alone and together, it wasn't about our intimacy that was helping us get to know each other better; it was something greater, which I didn't understand. When I saw my pretty wife walking towards the pool, it hit me that someone was telling me Charmaine was a perfect match in every sense, designed by God to be the ideal soul companion for me. We both had become of one essence, and were to enjoy unparalleled intimacy with each other, having been made for each other, but with a clear distinction in our earthly roles.

It hit me that I would no longer be alone.

Marriage is the celebration of daily commitment to each other. There would always be someone with me now when I awakened every morning, someone who belonged to me. I was beginning to see what life was all about. I was now a husband, a provider, and a protector. And someday a father. This awareness made me feel worthwhile at the age of nineteen years, soon to turn twenty the next month in July.

Charmaine was a sweet, innocent person at eighteen, who would turn nineteen in two months in September. Feeling proud, I got up and went to meet my soul mate at poolside.

A Rodeo came to town, and we spent an enjoyable evening watching the cowboys trying to stay on the bulls, along with all the other riders roping calves. The clowns put on a good show.

Driving around the area the next day, we were surprised to find an attractive restaurant on Lake Taneycomo that rented paddle boats, canoes, and row boats. We stopped and got out and went into a spacious foyer with varnished logged walls, couches and overstuff chars positioned on oriental rugs. There were hordes of children running around in bathing suits and others were covered with beach towels, tracking sand into the place, screaming at their parents to rent a paddle boat or canoe. I couldn't help but wonder where all the families came from. We didn't see this lodge listed in any of the literature we received when planning our honeymoon.

We had lunch and decided to rent a canoe. After spending most of the afternoon on the lake we decided to head back to our cottage.

CHAPTER 8

Returning from Our Honeymoon

We would now be living in my parents' home in a renovated upstairs attic area that had four rooms without walls. During our engagement period, I worked with a handyman my dad knew, who I assisted in putting up a wall for the room that converted into our bedroom and built a small bathroom next to the bedroom. In the area that could be the kitchen, we placed a breakfast set of table and chairs that my maternal grandparents gave us for a wedding present. It became my study area. One of the other areas facing the street we made into our living room.

We were fortunate that my folks allow us to live there rent-free and eat meals with them. The rest of the summer I worked again at East St. Louis Casting and Charmaine continued to work at Swift and Company.

With Charmaine's income and the money I earned during the summer, I was able to enroll at Washington University for the 1950-1951 school year. We couldn't afford a used car, so I had to ride the city bus to St. Louis and transfer to the Lindell bus that stopped in front of the university. It took ninety minutes one-way. I was at a disadvantage catching the five o'clock bus home. I couldn't go to the lab at night like the other students to look at slides, examining specimens in my biology courses. By the time I got home and ate my dinner, it was around 8 p.m. and I spent a couple of hours studying before I fell asleep on my books.

As a junior in the Spring of 1951, I had an unfortunate experience with Dr. Goldstien, my organic chemistry professor, who was also the upperclassmen's dean. I was sitting in the library studying for the next day's final organic exam when two of my friends came in and asked me how I did on the final. I thought they were kidding me but learned that they had just come out of it. I jumped up, heart racing a mile a minute, I ran across the quadrangle over to the chemistry building. Dr. Goldstien was standing outside the auditorium by the door collecting exams. I explained to him what had happened.

With a stern look, he said, "Tough."

"What? Can't I go in and try to take the exam?"

"Nope."

Frustrated, I said, "According to the student handbook, if I went to the Bursar's office and paid the fee, you would give me another exam."

"I don't care what the handbook says."

My frustration was mounting. "What about if I sat in your office and took the test with a grad student proctoring?"

"No."

"Okay. Then what is my option?"

"Retake the course this summer."

"You mean the lab and all?"

"Just the course, no lab. You'll get an incomplete for the semester."

I waddled away, wounded.

That summer of '51, I retook the organic course and after an exam, Dr. Goldstein said as he passed out the papers, "You're pretty good with the syntheses."

"I ought to be," I said. "You made me retake this course."

"Oh. You're the guy."

Yes, I'm the guy.

After the course was finished, I had only two months to work if I could find a job. I started to work at my old job at East St. Louis Casting, but it lasted for only two weeks, and I was laid off. Times were hard and the company had a layoff. I could only find a job working in Jones Park across from our home, which involved cleaning the rest rooms and picking up trash, and then sweeping the streets in the park. Fortunately, the job I had applied for at Hunter's Packing Company in the Stockyards opened and I was called to work after ten days at the park. Hunter's Packing paid well, and this allowed me to earn my tuition money.

The beginning of the Fall semester of 1951 at Wash U (that's what students called the university), I was fortunate to get a ride from one of Charmaine's girlfriend's husband who was an engineering student at the university. This made my life a little easier, but I still was not able to study in the lab at night.

CHAPTER 9
The Korean War

The day we got married, the Korean War started June 24, 1950, which was the 25th in Korea. In September 1951, I got a notice from my draft board in Belleville, Illinois, which ordered me to report in October to a military station in St. Louis, that I was being inducted into the Army.

Since I was married and in college before the war started, I knew I was entitled to a deferment. So, I wrote General Hershey in Chicago and stated my case. He wrote my draft board, and sent a copy to me, and ordered them to give me a deferment for one year. They sent me a letter indicating that I had the one-year deferment. After that year, I enrolled in classes the Fall of 1952 and would graduate with my B.A. in Chemistry. My draft board had other plans for me. I got another letter in September stating that in October 1952, I would report to the military operation in St. Louis. I appealed and went before the board. I based my case on being graduated if allowed to finish the school year. I could tell they were hacked off that I wrote General Hershey. I pleaded my case but sensed my words were falling on deaf ears. They denied my appeal. This meant that I had to drop out of school.

I went to my dean's office, Dean Goldstein, my old "friend," to drop out legally so not to get any bad grades. Goldstein told me he wouldn't take a million dollars for the time he spent in the Army during WWII and wouldn't take a million to go back. At least he wished me well.

34

I had a week before reporting to the military station in St. Louis for a physical and filling out all the paperwork.

Charmaine and I only had been married two years and never been apart. We had become very close. She cried every evening at the dinner table. Seated around the table were my mother and father, my grandma Struel, and Charmaine and me. We all looked at each other but said nothing, feeling what Charmaine was feeling. She and I had talked about plans for me to further my education after graduating from Washington University, but that wasn't going to happen. What was the future going to hold for us now?

Leaving Charmine after the week was over was heartbreaking. I could feel her shaking body as tears rolled down her face as we said goodbye.

I was sent to Fort Knox in Louisville, Kentucky, for basic training. After 12 weeks, I was being sent to Korea. I had a week at home before leaving for San Francisco on a train from St. Louis.

It was the worst week of my life.

I was going to be away from my bride for at least fifteen months. We were just getting to feel like one, as Scripture says. We felt so attached that we believed that God had brought us together. When my father and mother and Charmaine said goodbye to me at the train station in St. Louis, I felt like I was in a dream world. My heart was hurting, hugging my weeping wife. One consolation, Charmaine was going to live with my parents, who loved her very much and they would take good care of her. Also, my father was a physician. That made me feel much better. To see them walk off as I boarded the train, made me wonder if I would be seeing them again.

CHAPTER 10
On My Way to Korea

It took two days to get to Pittsburg, CA. Pittsburg is in the eastern part of Contra Costa County in San Francisco, and is 40 miles from SF. We got off the train and lined up on both sides of the tracks as the train pulled away, standing in the open fields from nowhere. Hundreds of us looked around, wondering what was happening. Soon a series of yellow school buses, driven by Mexican drivers, pulled up on the opposite side of the tracks and we were instructed to board and were taken to a camp where we bunked for several days until we were bussed to the docks and boarded a ferry which took us to a navy ship, the U.S.S. Breckenridge. In the lower level of the ship were bunks, three strong white broadcloth with bars on the sides, stacked one on top of the other. I had the upper bunk, close to the latrine.

We all were on top deck when the ship left San Francisco Bay, standing at the railings looking at the city fading away in the background.

They were thinking the same as I.

Will we be coming home alive?

Several days later we pulled into the port of Honolulu, Hawaii for a day. We were allowed to leave the ship for several hours, and I spent that time walking around the town and bought something to mail back to Charmaine.

It took a total of 14 days to reach the port of Yokohama, south of

Tokyo, Japan from Hawaii. We deboarded and were bussed to a train station where we traveled for several hours to a camp to pick up new clothing and our rifles.

We again boarded the train the next morning, returning to the port to board a Merchant Marine ship that was completely different from the navy ship. This ship didn't have the amenities of the Navy ship, and the mariners came above board less frequently than the sailors. The ship appeared to be a floating ghost ship with hundreds of soldiers up top. It was a little eerie. It took us several days to enter the area of Inchon, Korea. We went down the ship's gangplank onto an LST, still not close to the land, which moved us toward the harbor. On the way, we passed another LST that was loaded with GIs who had served their time and were heading home.

These GIs were hollering at us: "Fresh meat! The Chinks are waiting for you guys!" And they were laughing it up and waving. I know they were extremely happy to be going home but telling us the enemy was waiting for us didn't help our spirits. Our LST dropped its front panel to the ground, and we hurried off, moving about twenty yards on land where there was a throng of activity—a multitude of military allies. I stepped on Korean soil on May 01, 1953. Military units from all over the world were preparing to return to their countries. I distinctly remember a group of African soldiers loading heavy wooden boxes of rifles on a transport. They had long arms, and they picked up the box with such ease, like it was a box of food.

In about an hour we boarded a train with small cattle cars and traveled several days up north to a large camp. It was a camp where GIs came in from all over and were assigned to different Divisions of the military throughout Korea. I was assigned to the 40th Infantry Division, a California National Guard, the Division Surgeon General's Office.

CHAPTER 11
Surgeon General's Office: 40th Infantry Division

After two weeks, six of us were transported 65 miles north of the 38th parallel, in a deuce-and-half-ton military truck, riding in the back wearing green fatigues and carrying our weapons and duffle bags. The ride was rough traveling over dusty roads up and down several hills. I was dropped off at the entrance of the 40th Infantry Division Headquarters. The camp was six miles behind front lines, and it consisted of many tents housing all the major offices in the Division. In addition, we had an aid station, motor pool, and living tents spread over acres surrounded by hills over which our F-80 or F-86A jets zoomed heading to the front lines.

I reported in at the Division Surgeon's office, where I met the Division Surgeon, a Colonel. I was introduced to a lieutenant, staff sergeant and a corporal, who took me to a tent that I would occupy with six other G.I.s to deposit my duffle bag and my M-1 rifle. Later it was exchanged in Quarter Master for a Carbine, which was much easier to carry around.

For several nights I had a hard time with homesickness. I missed Charmaine terribly. I had to tell myself that I couldn't function if I let the memories get to me. I reminded myself that she was well taken care of, living with my family. My folks had no daughters, just three boys. So, they took to Charmaine and my father was a physician, so that helped me get though my battle. I wrote her a letter every night.

We were six miles behind the lines and at dusk we would hear "boom, boom, boom" all night long. The field artillery would start shooting off at that time. The war was fought only at dusk and through the night. After a while I got used to all the booms at night. The only fear we had was listening at night for "Bed Check, Charlie," who flew over at night in the area dropping a bomb. How he ever got through the lines, I don't know. Fortunately, I never heard the engine of his plane fly over our camp.

Besides looking over medical records in the Division, my job was to call for helicopters at MASH (just like on TV) to fly up to the line to pick up the traumatic wounded, which meant those who had arms or legs blown off from stepping on land mines. The medics would call me with coordinates, and I called MASH to relay the position. I went to MASH once with the Medical Officer and went into surgery where the surgeons were sewing up a G.I. who had lost both legs. The surgery didn't bother me, but seeing the soldier lying there rips your heart out. All I could think about was his pain and what his future was going to be, returning to the States at Walter Reed and meeting his wife and children or his family. The image stayed with me for several days. From time to time, I wondered how he was. I hoped he was doing well, and I prayed for him,

We distributed Chloroquine to everyone for the prevention of malaria. And our clothing and socks had to be dipped often into a solution to prevent the bite of a tick that caused Hemorrhagic Fever. This disease was the worst and could be very devastating. It caused bleeding from every orifice in the body. GIs who contacted Hemorrhagic Fever had to be flown by helicopter to a special treatment unit.

At the time when the Staff Sergeant and the other Sergeant in our office rotated home, my rank was corporal, and I was promoted to Sergeant. The Lieutenant was the assistant medical officer to the Division Surgeon, who we only called "The Colonel." (I don't remember his name, but he was from Chillicothe, Illinois, my home state). One early June morning I had to drive the Lieutenant up to the front lines to check over the sanitary conditions where the Commander had complained that the ROK (Republic of Korea) troops were defecating in the trenches, causing a health hazard. I drove six miles over rough terrain, over hills, and down into Chorwon Valley, where the 224th Battalion was stationed. The valley was believed sacred because the Chinese never launched any shells into it. At battalion, we received our bullet-proof vests, steel helmets, and carbines and then headed up the mountain. It was cold up there. After fifteen minutes we reached the unit. I visited with the medics by their bunker while the Lieutenant met with the Commanding officer. While we were standing outside the bunker talking with the medics, a blast came in. I hit the dirt. They, laughing at me, forgot to tell me the engineers were blasting a road in the side of a mountain. Well, we were trained to hit the dirt, and I did just that. They didn't make a joke of it. They knew what had happened. I felt foolish, but not too much. I was happy when we returned to the Division. It was cold up there and dreary. It would take some getting used to.

The war ended on my birthday, July 27, 1953. We were ordered to move the entire Division miles west of where we were and reset the entire camp up, which took days. During the months that followed, I bunked with five other G.I.s in a large tent. I was called several times by the Company Clerk to go for a week on R & R to Japan. I declined. I told him, "I wasn't leaving Korea until I was called to go home." Some of the guys who went on a R&R came back depressed, moaned and groaned about being back because being in Japan was like being stateside. They couldn't understand why I didn't want to leave this hell hole. I told them, "You guys walk around for a week like zombies. I'm married and I'm not leaving here until I'm called to go home."

When the 40th Infantry Division rotated home in early spring of 1954, I couldn't go with them because I didn't have enough points. So, I was reassigned to an aid station in the Third Armored Division.

The Aid Station Sergeant didn't take to me. I believe he didn't like a Sergeant First Class GI coming into his aid station. I was there for three months, and I avoided him, but he thought he was going to show me who was boss. There was going to be an inspection in two days outside the aid station close to an incline. During an inspection we would place our equipment at our feet and stand at attention when the colonel came down each row to inspect us. I didn't have time to clean my equipment nor was I going to. Sergeants don't stand for the inspection, but I was ordered to. The day came and dozens of us were forming rows as we saw the colonel get out of his jeep. The other GIs were giving me a stare wondering what a Sergeant was doing in line. I was first in my row and when the Colonel came up to me, I stood at attention.

He said, "Sergeant, what the hell are you doing here?"

I said, "Sir, the aid station Sergeant put me on the list and wouldn't remove my name."

"Get your things and leave us. You don't belong here, Sergeant."

"Yes, sir. Thank you, sir."

I grabbed my stuff and took off to my tent to deposit everything.

Later that day I got the call from the Company Clerk that I was waiting for. He said, "Magarian, this isn't about R&R. Tomorrow morning at eight be in front of the aid station. You're going home and I'm going with you."

Talk about being on cloud nine, I threw things into my duffle bag and wrote a short letter telling Charmaine I'm leaving in the morning (I don't remember the actual date) and coming home. I didn't sleep much that night.

Charmaine with her friend Faye Cleveland

Bob sent flowers at Easter in 1954

Bob sent flowers on their 4th Anniversary

CHAPTER 12
Homeward Bound: Thank God!

The next morning the company clerk and I hopped into a jeep that took us about ten miles to an open area of acres and acres of land with only one set of railroad tracks running through it. We were ordered to stand by the tracks in assigned groups. Got the word we were going way down to Pusan, which would take a couple of days.

Who cared. We were going home.

A train that must have been resurrected from its graveyard finally arrived. The cars were old and rusty and inside the wooden seats faced each other. The cars were small, hadn't seen anything like them before. Two of us sat in a seat facing two other GIs. Our seats were next to a window that we could open. It took two days and plenty of C-rations to get to Pusan. As we pulled into the area where army trucks were waiting for us, civilians were walking by the side of our train. They smiled and seemed glad we were there. We were taken to a nearby camp where we were processed and given physicals in their medical unit. After one night, we were transported to the navy yard the next afternoon where a troop ship was docked. We hopped out of the trucks with our duffle bags and lined up in formation along the dock eagerly waiting to board the big ship which had *USS Mann* painted on the side.

Everyone was laughing and in high spirits. We were so eager to board the ship. We're going home. Finally! That's what was on our minds. We couldn't believe it. After about ten minutes, we heard from a loudspeaker, an officer called out: "Sergeant First Class Magarian report to the ship's guard station." Being surprised doesn't describe my emotions at the time. I grabbed my duffle bag and hurried up the gangplank and entered. I was struck how bright everything was inside the ship. White was painted throughout, and it felt clean. For 15 months of being exposed only to green—vehicles, tents, our clothes— the brightness felt grand.

I reported to the officer inside the guard station. I was handed a sheet that gave me instructions, stating that I was to be Sergeant of the Guard and would march a group of eight men twice a day to respective stations on the ship for them to stand guard. This was not only a troop ship, but officers' families were on board, and we had to protect them. I was told to go to quarters and settle in, which meant—find a bunk and put your stuff away. Since there were very few soldiers on the ship, I had my pick for a lower bunk close to the latrine. I took a shower in hard water but was happy to be there.

The ship pulled away on my birthday, July 27, 1954. I turned 24 years old. The best present I ever received or will ever receive!

Going home to Charmaine, my dear wife.

For the twelve days we were on the USS Mann, I met the eight men outside the guard's station and had them fall in line, then marched them around the ship on the level with the families, and one-by-one, a soldier stepped out of formation to replace the guard on duty, who joined our ranks and we marched to the next station, and finally back to the guard station.

The day we were moving into the port of Portland, Oregon, we all were at our bunks dressing into our dress uniforms. One of the men who was in my guard group was standing by his bunk near me dressing up. When I put on my shirt and he saw my stripes, he said,

"Man, you a Sergeant First Class?"

I said, "Yeah, so what?"

He shook his head and said, "Man, I can't believe it. You're so nice and you associated with us the whole time."

He was a corporal.

"I'm still the same guy, stripes or no stripes."

He shook his head again, "You the man," he said.

We clasped hands and both said in unison, "We're home!"

We were ordered on top deck to stand in formation and then dismissed to watch as the ship docked in port.

As I looked over the coastline of Portland, a tingling sensation came over my entire body, realizing we were home—the greatest country in the world. Tears filled my eyes. I thought, how lucky I am to be home, but there were those of my brothers who didn't make it. God's blessing be with them and their families. I figuratively fell to my knees.

Thank you, Lord for our safe return!

When we left the ship heading down the gangplank, we were met by Red Cross ladies who gave us some goodies and welcomed us home. I could have kissed them and was tempted to kiss the ground. I couldn't wait to call home. It was 2:00 p.m. local time, and back home in Illinois it was 4:00 p.m. Charmaine was at work.

They loaded us on buses and took us to a camp where we were told to go into the barracks and wait until we were called to go to the airport. Inside were bunks with the mattresses rolled up and their springs exposed. We just stood around waiting to be transported to the airport, sitting on our duffle bags. But I had to find a phone. I searched and finally found one and called home. My dad answered and he was excited to hear my voice. It felt good to hear his, too. I told him to call Charmaine at work and tell her I'm home, and that we will be leaving Portland soon, flying to Chicago. We will be taken to Camp Sheridan early tomorrow afternoon.

He said he, Mom and Charmaine would meet me at Camp Sheridan.

CHAPTER 13
Flying to Chicago: Discharge from The Army

We boarded our bus to the airport. Behind the driver was an African-American soldier, who asked if we were going to board one of those big airplanes to fly home in.

The driver said, "Oh, yes. Where I'm taking you, you'll have one of those big guys."

The soldier was all smiles and very entertaining. When the bus pulled into the airport the driver took us around the side road away from the large planes and pulled in behind a small building. Parked next to the building was a "Flying Tigers" Douglas DC-3 prop plane.

The soldier said, "I thought you said we were going to have one of those big ones."

The driver laughed. "That's big enough for you guys."

Flying Tigers fought in WWII and now were in the airline business. The DC-3 only flew 192 miles an hour and had a range of 1495 miles.

We deboarded the bus and stood behind the shack and waited. A stewardess opened the plane's back door and waved us on. She greeted each one of us with a smile as we boarded. It didn't look very big inside, but who cared. We were going home. We found our seats and tried to get comfortable. The African American soldier was seated on an aisle seat two rows in front of me, and when the pilot and copilot came on board, the soldier jumped up in front of the pilots and said, "Sir, if you have any trouble up there, will you call me?"

Everyone laughed.

The captain said, "Son, if we have any trouble, you'd be the first one wanted out of here. Have a seat and we'll get you home."

We took off around dusk and flew through the night, stopping off around five in the morning for some snacks and fuel. When the pilot moved to the runway and gunned the engines for takeoff, the soldier was hollering as the plane raced down the runway.

"Lift this baby, Oh, Oh. I don't want my wife to get my insurance."

He kept hollering, "Ooh, ooh, get this baby up."

There was a fence at the end of the runway. "Get it up, up," he yelled. "We made it. She ain't gonna get my insurance."

We enjoyed his humor.

We arrived in Chicago in early afternoon on the 12th of August, boarded several buses to Camp Sheridan, and were dropped off at a building where we would receive our separation papers. We had served our 2 years of active duty, but now had a six-year inactive duty obligation. It took about two hours for us to be processed and receive our papers, and then moved into a large room with folding chairs. I chose a seat in the front row near the aisle. Our group filled half the room.

A Colonel entered and began talking to us about a future with the Army. If we signed up, we'd get a month's leave, and for those of us who weren't interested, he talked about our obligations in the six years of inactive duty. No way would I re-enlist. I was going back to college.

While in Korea, I met this Lieutenant who came often to the Surgeon General's office. He and I hit it off when he learned I was from East St. Louis. He was from Jerseyville, Illinois, up north from my hometown. He asked what I was going to do after I got out of the Army. I told him I was going back to college, but hadn't decided on one yet, that Wash U. was too expensive. And now that I would get the G.I. bill, we were planning on moving away from home. I had checked with Purdue and Indiana University, looking for married housing. They only had trailer courts. He asked me if I had ever thought of going south. I had not. He said he went to Ole Miss because they have married housing, called Vets Village. It consisted of Army barracks from WWII that were converted into apartment units. He said he paid $19 a month for a two-bedroom apartment while he was in Pharmacy School. I wrote the University of Mississippi and got their bulletins and admission requirements. I wrote Charmaine and asked if she minded going to Ole Miss. She didn't. So, I applied and had all my transcripts sent. They accepted me in the premed program for the fall class of 1954.

While the Colonel was speaking, I heard some voices in the back. I turned to look over my left shoulder, and to my happy surprise, there were my mother and father and Charmaine talking to the Corporal guarding the back area where there were many family members seated in the chairs waiting, too. My heart was pounding seeing my lovely wife again, only a few yards away. When we were dismissed, I hurried to the back to the open arms of my sweet wife, then my mother and father.

It was such a relief to be back home with Charmaine again. When we embraced, I got a warm loving feeling to be back in Charmaine's arms again.

The Corporal smiled and said, "Welcome home, Sergeant." Later, I learned that Charmaine had to restrain herself from rushing up front. The Corporal told her she had to wait in the back like the others, that I'd be dismissed soon.

As we left the building, we decided to stay the night in the hotel on the base, which was only a couple of blocks away. Since there were many soldiers with families, my folks decided they'd not take a room from the soldiers. They would find a place in town.

Charmaine and I had our second honeymoon that day. It felt like a dream being with my bride again. I couldn't believe I was home. Anywhere in the U.S. would be home after spending 15 months isolated from civilization—living in green tents, seeing only hills, green army vehicles, soldiers dressed in green fatigues, and freezing weather. I felt like I had been living on the moon.

The next day, my mother met us in their red Oldsmobile in front of the hotel. She got out and I got behind the steering wheel and Charmaine in the passenger seat, while my folks rode in the back. As we were leaving, it was sunset and I heard the bugles for Retreat, which marks the end of the workday, and is accompanied by a ceremonious lowering of the base colors and the U.S. flag. I pulled over to the curb, got out, and noticed several cars stopped behind me. We stood at attention and saluted the colors of the flag. I got back into the car and noticed the smiles on everyone's face. I believe they were proud of me.

We left the camp and headed to Racine, Wisconsin to visit family. Being with family felt good. We stayed a couple of days and then headed home to East St. Louis. Felt strange to be back in my hometown. Life was slowly returning to normal. We stayed for a week visiting Charmaine's folks and enjoying a welcoming home party my folks gave for me. I was happy to see Grandma Struel again, who lived with us after Grandpa Oscar died in 1948. Before we left for Mississippi, I went up to the Draft Board in Belleville, the town in which I attended the junior college in the late '40s. I went to inform the board that I was back so they could make some kind of entry, which I forgot what it was. I asked if they remembered me when I told them they took me out of Wash U. One person said, "Oh, you're the one." I said under my breath, "Yeah, I'm the one." They welcomed me back home. Which didn't impress me.

Bob & Charmaine celebrating his return at her folks

Bob & Charmaine with her brothers and sister

CHAPTER 14
Visiting Ole Miss

This Monday morning in August 1954, Charmaine and I hopped into our used Plymouth coupe that we had purchased six months before I went into the Army and drove south to the University of Mississippi (Ole Miss). We planned to look over the campus and check in with housing. We drove a route through southern Illinois down through the western tip of Kentucky and Tennessee and into Mississippi. Once in the state, we saw cotton fields filled with workers. Never saw anything like it except in the movies. As we headed to Oxford from Holly Springs, we entered the city on Lamar Road, which ran perpendicularly into the square. We went around the west side of the white building in the center of the square onto Lamar and stopped at a red light a half-block south of the square. Lamar bisected University Avenue that ran east and west. I felt something seemed strange about the downtown part around the square but didn't know what it was until later.

Oxford had a literary beginning with Nobel Prize winning author William Faulkner, who used the town as the inspiration for the county seat of his fictional Yoknapatawpha County. The literature we received from the University revealed that his antebellum home, Rowan Oak, where he wrote many of his masterpieces, was located close to the campus.

At the light we turned right on University Avenue, passing beautiful southern homes for three blocks and reaching the Mary Buie Museum a half block from the Oxford High School on the left and a Roman Catholic Church on the right and then came upon a small bridge high over railroad tracks and entered the campus of Ole Miss. The first thing that caught our eye was the beautiful Grove to our right. Instead of going straight, we took the loop to the right that circled the Grove. I remembered reading about it in the literature we received. It covers ten acres filled with magnolias, elms and oaks. Oxford is a big football town in the SEC, and on any Saturday home game, the Grove is filled with dozens and dozens of cars. Hundreds of Ole Miss Rebel tailgaters come, filling the Grove with students, alumni, and fans.

We drove onward until we came into a circle that looped around an island called "The Circle." There was a flagpole in the center surrounded by many trees.

Beautiful.

To our right was the Lyceum Building, a Greek Revival brick building with six columns. This building housed the Chancellor's office and other administrative officials. The literature stated that the Lyceum Building was the first building erected on the Ole Miss campus and was used as a Confederate hospital during the Civil War. We drove around The Circle with an American Flag in the middle looking at all the buildings.

Coming on campus from the bridge and not turn around the Grove, the first thing noticeable about The Circle is a Confederate Statue prominently positioned at its edge close to the street. A sidewalk dissected the island heading up to the Lyceum Building.

Another sidewalk crisscrossed its center at the flagpole where students could walk to and from classes from the north side to the south side and vice versa. Traffic could only go one way—traveling around the right side of The Circle and head out on the other side toward the bridge. The buildings surrounding the island starting on the right side were: Ventress Hall, the Y (behind it was the Barnard Observatory), Fine Arts, Fulton Chapel, Peabody, and the Lyceum Administration building, and heading out on other side were: Chemistry/Pharmacy, Carrier Hall of Engineering, and the Science (Biology) building, and then back to the bridge and toward town on University Avenue.

We parked in an open spot at The Circle across from the Lyceum.

The weather was pleasant for late August. We went up the concrete steps and walked between the columns to two eight-foot white doors that were heavy and took some effort to open. We entered and walked down the shiny tile linoleum hallway, hoping to find someone to direct us to the Student Housing Office, since we didn't get directions in the mail. We didn't see any secretaries or Admission offices, so we continued to the end of the hall facing another set of monstrous white doors. Suddenly a middle-aged man dressed in rolled up sleeves and slacks came out of the office to our left.

He asked, "How can I help you folks?"

I noticed the sign on his door, William Alton Bryant, *Vice-Chancellor*.

I responded, "Sir, we're looking for the Married Student Housing Office."

"Come this way," he said, as he walked us to the big doors, opened them and motioned for us to step out. Across the street was the library.

He pointed, "See that building over there to the right of the library?"

"Yes, sir," Charmaine and I said in unison.

"Go in there and tell Mr. Bailey that Dr. Bryant sent you and he'll take care of you."

We thanked him and headed to the building. I immediately was reminded how I'd never see the vice-presidents at Wash U. They were like ghosts. I even had to make appointments to see my course professors. You couldn't walk in and ask for help without an appointment. Already I was getting good vibes about this University.

Very impressed.

We found Mr. Bailey, who was also very friendly and helpful. He gave us a small map and keys to a downstairs two-bedroom apartment in Vet's Village. We walked over to our car and took off, following the map to Vets Village. Behind the row of fraternity houses were nothing but white, double story framed buildings. Each building was numbered, and we found our building, pulled up by the steps and parked. We entered the building. Our unit was on the right and there was one on our left. I looked up the stairs and noticed two entrances across from each other, just like where we were standing. I opened the door to our unit, which led into the living room. To the left were a small kitchen and bathroom. We walked past the bathroom and through the door with a small hall and a small bedroom to our left and walked into the larger bedroom to our right. There were small closets in each room but very little storage space. All rooms were painted off-white, making the rooms seem larger. The only disadvantage was the heating unit inside used kerosene, which had to be transported in five-gallon cans from the 50-gallon drum on the side of the building. I could see I would have some cold days in the winter. But who could complain for $19 per month?

We locked up the unit and headed back to tell Mr. Bailey we would take the unit and signed the papers. Across from Mr. Bailey's building and behind the library was the Student Union, in which were a bookstore, clothing store, concession stand, a large fast-food grill, and a post office. Char and I walked in to get a P.O. Box.

We drove around the campus to get acquainted with more of the buildings. Our plan was to stay another day and then head back home. I was thrilled that now I would be able to go to the lab at night as often as needed, since the main campus buildings were only five minutes from Vets Village.

We went back to the square, and checked into the Holiday Inn on north Lamar, a couple of blocks from the square, and rested for a couple of hours. We then rode around and had dinner at a local restaurant. During dinner I was reading the booklet the hotel clerk gave me about all the famous sites in Oxford. I wanted to make sure we saw enough before leaving. I was particularly interested in seeing William Faulkner's home. After dinner, we decided to rest for the evening and do our touring the next morning. While resting in our room, I couldn't get the thought out of my mind about something being unusual about the town. *What was it?* I asked Charmaine if she knew what I was talking about. She didn't. As I was about to get under the covers, I turned to her and said, "I know what it is! There are no taverns or saloons in this town. Back home there's one on every corner."

We rose the next morning around eight, got dressed and before we left to return to our car for a day of sightseeing, I thought I'd ask the clerk why there were no bars or taverns in Oxford. He was a student at Ole Miss (the university's nickname), smiled, and said, "Sir, Mississippi is a dry state."

He saw the frown on my face and said, "No alcoholic beverages are sold legally in Mississippi."

I looked at Charmaine and she smiled at me.

"What do you mean, legally?" I said, turning back to him, knowing what it really meant, but wanted to hear it from him. *Bootlegging or speakeasies,* I thought. He smiled, again, "You Yankees don't know the tricks we have up our sleeves, but down here there are ways around the law. We can get beer in certain counties. But you must know which counties and where to go."

"I see," I said, returning a smile. "Thanks."

Back in our Plymouth we began our sightseeing tour. I learned from the brochure that the Oxford population in 1954 was around 4000 and the square was the main attraction besides the University, its Grove, and Rowan Oak, William Faulkner's estate.

In the center of the square was The Lafayette County Courthouse. Across the street on the south side of the Courthouse was Blaylock's Drug store on the corner of south Lamar and Van Buren. Several doors west of the Blaylock's on Van Buren was Gathright and Reed Pharmacy, and several doors east of Blaylock's was New's Pharmacy. Behind the Courthouse in the north direction was Leslie's Drug Store on Jackson Ave. There was a Post office on the corner of Jackson and east of the courthouse. We parked in front of Leslie's Drug Store and went in for a cup of coffee and a light breakfast. Then we decided to walk around this historic Square looking into every shop. We ended up in one of the icons on the east side of the square, Neilson's Department Store, an Oxford institution, the oldest department store in the south. The place had the smell of department stores back home. We had money, but our goal was to save it for our Ole Miss days. Of course, we had to buy a few things to take home with us.

We walked back to our car with a few packages and drove south of the Square looking for Rowen Oaks, William Faulkner's estate on Old Taylor Road. We found it and pulled in on a chat road for about twenty feet where we met a closed, locked gate that had a *Private Property* sign on it. We got out of the car and went to the gate and stood, looking down the long row of very tall cedar trees that lined the side of the walkway that seemed to go for fifty yards to the front of a two-story white antebellum mansion with columns. The brochure contained interesting information about Rowen Oak. It added that Faulker purchased the home in 1930. The plants and landscape are where Faulkner walked and tended during the writing of his novels. It revealed that he saw and smelled the earth and listened to the sounds from the cultivated grounds and surrounding woods. I remembered from my courses that he was well known for his novels: *The Sound and the Fury, As I Lay Dying, Sanctuary,* and *Absalom, Absalom.*

We were hoping to see Mr. Faulkner walking the property. There was no one. The clerk at the hotel said we may not see him; he spends some time in Virginia. After about an hour we decided to go back to the Square and have dinner and then call it a day. We had an early departure the next morning for our trip back home.

Lyceum Building

The Circle

William Faulkner's home

CHAPTER 15
Enrolling at Ole Miss

After arriving back home in East St. Louis, we began packing our things and hired a moving company. While packing, I could see sadness in my mother's and father's eyes, and they were somewhat quiet. I figured they would miss us since I hadn't been home from Korea but for only four weeks and was now leaving again. I learned that my dad was sad because I was taking their card playing partner from them. Charmaine had told me all the things she had done with her friend, Faye Cleveland, and my mom while I was away. One happy thing they did religiously was playing cards every evening after supper.

Well, it *seems he'll miss Charmaine more than I.*   -

The moving van came, and our plan was to leave the next day. The workers finished packing all our things in a few hours. The next morning when it was time for us to leave, I got a little emotional. We hugged and Charmaine was in tears, and I nearly was, too. It was like I was leaving for the Army again.

We arrived in Oxford before the moving van had arrived. Looking around inside our unit, I was reminded of the barracks I had lived in while in the Army, except the space inside this one was divided into rooms. While waiting for the movers, we met our neighbors across from us. Jimmy and Anna Ray Gassaway had a baby girl, Marion. Jimmy was a student in Engineering. I felt we were going to become good friends.

After the moving van arrived, we began arranged the furniture as they brought everything in. The place was starting to take shape and didn't look so bad. Good enough for a couple who were in school and not planning on doing a lot of entertaining. We had our bedroom set, sheets, pillowcases, blankets, a couch for the living room and a small console TV, and a Formica kitchen table with six chairs, dinner plates and silverware for six. The small bedroom would remain empty since we had no more furniture, but it could be used for storage for what little we had.

While in the service I had most of my pay sent home to Charmaine, who banked it with a portion of her earnings. We were required to keep ten dollars for personal items, shaving cream and toothpaste. I was a smoker and cigarettes in Korea were $1.00 per carton (ten cents a pack). I quit smoking before I returned home.

I was on the GI bill now and we had our savings from my time in Korea and Charmaine's savings that would supplement my GI income. It was fortunate that we had the savings because our second-hand Plymouth had seen its better days. We learned from our neighbor that the Chevrolet dealer in Holly Springs was having a big sale on all its cars. We went and found the dealership and after some haggling, we were able to get the deal we wanted on a 1954, four-door green and white Chevrolet. We suspected we got the deal because the car had a four-barrel carburetor, and we sensed that the farmers didn't want the car.

During my enrollment in the pre-med program, I was told I needed a double minor. At Wash U. I only needed a major and a minor. This meant that instead of receiving my degree in one year, it would take two years. I wouldn't graduate until June 1956. My major was Philosophy and Chemistry was my minor, so I chose Biology as my second minor. I chose Philosophy so I could learn other things outside of the chemical and biological sciences.

It took a couple of weeks to get used to the campus and town, but I loved the place because the Chemistry Building was across the street from the Lyceum building and two building down from chemistry was the Biology Building. No traffic and I was only five minutes from our apartment. Compared to St. Louis, I was in heaven.

For the first month Charmaine dealt with homesickness. She had never been away from home. Our neighbor, Anna Ray Gassaway, who stayed home with her baby girl, Marion, became a great friend of Charmaine and they visited during the day, which helped Charmaine adjust. We enjoyed getting together with Jimmy and Anna Ray on weekends and were introduced to southern pastries that were out of this world.

During the summer of 1955, Joe and Doris Allen moved upstairs over our apartment. Joe was a graduate student in physical chemistry. They joined our group, and we all became very close. During that summer my brother Ed, who was five years younger than I, was attending St. Louis University, came to spend a week with us. We were wondering if he would come to school at Ole Miss, but he didn't like it here.

The two-year medical school was on the Ole Miss campus prior to 1953, when it moved to Jackson and became a four-year medical school. I acquired information and an application from the dean's office.

In December 1955 we learned that Charmaine was pregnant with our first child, who was expected to join us the next year in September. In January 1956, I applied to the medical school for the Fall class of 1957. Somehow, I overlooked that they only took Mississippi residents. I talked with the Dean, hoping that as a graduate of Ole Miss, I would get in, but I was told if I stayed out one year after graduation, they'd take me in the Fall class of 1957. I told the Dean we were moving to Jackson, and I'd stay in touch. We then made plans to move to Jackson after graduation and I'd look for a job for a year.

Charmaine & Bob in their apartment living room at Ole Miss

Charmaine & Anna Ray
Gassaway & Marion

Bob & Jimmy Gassaway

Jimmy & Anna Ray

CHAPTER 16
Our Move to Jackson, MS

In Spring 1956, I got a call from Hydig, who said Ed wanted to come and live with us. What did we think? I was surprised and said, "I thought he didn't like it here."

I learned that Ed was tired of driving to St. Louis every day and wanted to get away from home. He only had one more year to get his BS in chemistry. I told Hydig I'd discuss it with Charmaine and get back with him.

There wasn't much discussion because she said it would be fine. So, Ed came with us in June of 1956, when we were getting ready to move to Raymond Gardens in Jackson. We enjoyed his company, and I was getting to know him more since I was in the army while he was in high school. He initiated plans to attend Millsaps College in Jackson and was accepted into one of the finest schools in the state to complete his chemistry degree.

We moved into a two-bedroom apartment in Raymond Gardens, located on the south side of Jackson, about ten miles from downtown. The Gardens was a nice little village of apartments. Once settled in, Charmaine and I began looking for jobs. She got a secretarial position in a Real Estate office owned by a very nice couple. She worked there up to five days before delivering our first child.

I went to the new medical school building searching for a job with Dr. Arthur Guyton, a physiologist, well known for his expertise and his

Textbook of Medical Physiology, which quickly became the standard. Dr. Guyton got his BA from Ole Miss and his MD from Harvard. His textbook is the world's best -selling medical physiology textbook and is translated in 15 languages. He was the head of the University of Mississippi Dept. of Physiology and Biophysics. I admired him because in reading his bio, where I learned he never succumbed to the crippling effects of polio and went on to accomplish so much.

I entered the main entrance of the medical school building that had been opened three years earlier. I immediately noticed how new everything was in the lobby, and the place even had a smell of newness. I approached the receptionist sitting behind a semicircle desk. I learned Dr. Guyton was on the third floor. I walked to the bank of elevators and to my surprise, there was the man, waiting for the elevator door to open. He stood patiently between two metal crutches that had semicircle metal braces for his upper arms and protruding out in the middle were handles for his hands.

He looked at me and asked, "Are you Bob Magarian?"

Shocked, I said, "Yes, sir."

We entered the elevator, I behind him. He pushed the button for the third floor. "I'm Arthur Guyton. Pleased to meet you, Bob."

"Thank you, sir," I said. "Pleased to meet you, sir."

I followed him into his lab, which, like all research labs, look alike with lab benches covered with special equipment. He had many students in his group of researchers.

He ushered me into his adjacent office. He waved a hand for me to sit, and he moved to his chair behind his desk after slipping out of the crutches. "I appreciate the material you dropped off with my secretary." I nodded.

He was very kind and thoughtful and as he looked over my resume, I knew it wasn't good from his demeanor. He looked up at me and in a kind voice so as not to hurt my feelings, he said he couldn't use me because I didn't have enough research experience. I knew right away when he took me into his lab I was out of my league. He had an inventive mind. Built most of the equipment in his lab. I learned that his dad was an ophthalmologist, and this Dr. Arthur Guyton had 10 children, all of whom were well-educated and had gone to med school and become specialists. I realized then I couldn't do very much with my BA degree.

I got a job for three months at one of the best department stores in Jackson—The Emporium—for the Holiday season. I first worked the third floor in the sheet and bedding department, where I was assigned to fill and decorate an area with all the Christmas toys and dolls. I had the helpers bring up all the boxes from storage and I went to work with a lady who was very helpful. We arranged all the toys and dolls in such a way that even I was surprised. I learned one thing about myself. I liked taking charge of a project to see the end results. After that I went to work in the shirt department on the first floor with another part-timer who did a funny thing. A lady came in and asked him what she could get her husband for Christmas, a man that had everything. My buddy said, "Get him a box to put it all in." We all got a big laugh, even the lady, and then he found something for her.

After the holidays, I was let go. I then took a position with the IRS, working on the third floor of the Federal Building processing tax returns. It wasn't long before I learned about the government, which I didn't like. The floor I worked on was filled with dozens of women and there was just one other man and I, who were part-timers.

Our supervisor was a lady who I liked. She was kind and fair. One thing I saw and didn't like was many of the women were snooty behind the super's back. Our super went on her lunch hour every Friday to get her hair done. She and her husband liked to go dancing. I thought she looked very nice. The women around me began saying condescending things about her. I was disappointed in a couple of them, some of whom I liked. They were saying how the super thought she was hot stuff parading around all dressed up.

I told them, "She looks very attractive, and I thought it was good of her to want to look pretty for her husband." Well, that didn't go over very well. They just shrugged off my comments. I couldn't wait for the day when I was scheduled to leave.

There was one tragic incident I'll never forget. I came to know a lady in another department through her son. He came often to see his mother and we got to know each other from our conversation in the coffee room. He was about my age and very interesting to talk to. He went to New Orleans and during the Mardi Gras he was killed in an auto accident. When I learned of it, all I could think of was: *his poor mother*. My heart ached for him and his mother. I thought I'd try and comfort her when she returned.

A couple weeks later, when I heard she was back, I got up the nerve to go see her. She had a 9 X 10 photograph of her son on her desk. She looked at me and smiled but the eyes were sad. I felt uncomfortable, not knowing what to say, but knew I had to give her my condolences and tell her how sorry I was. That I really enjoyed her son and my conversations with him. She was pleased to see me and to tell me about her son as if I hadn't known him. I could see a mother's love and how her loss had taken a toll. She appeared so broken- hearted. I went to see her a few times before I left. I noticed how withdrawn she had become. I didn't know what it was like to lose a son, but later in life I was going to find out.

Charmaine & Ed

Charmaine & Bob

CHAPTER 17
Birth of Our First Child: Paula Marie

During her pregnancy, Charmaine's feet were swollen and she had to get sandals. One sunny afternoon, she washed them and put them on our back porch to dry. We looked all over for them.

Out front, we saw our neighbor standing in the street with his son, pointing into the drain. I figured his 11-year-old boy snuck up that afternoon and grabbed the shoes and took off, and then had thrown them into the sewer in front of our apartment that was covered with a grid-iron lid. The boy's dad apparently saw what his son had done, because he stood by while he made the boy go down into the hole to get the sandals. We all stood around like hunters gazing into the opening, watching as the boy went down. The opening was clear, and the drain had no water in it. He was safe down there. The little guy came up and slammed the sandals at the edge of the drain. We helped him out and gave him a big hug. Then we all laughed about what he had done.

We made several trips to the new hospital that was built along with the medical school—opened in 1955—to see her doctor. The new hospital was very clean and attractive. Charmaine's ob-gyn doctor was Dr. Michael Newton, head of the Department of Obstetrics and Gynecology. He wasn't the friendliest doctor, but a good one. Charmaine worked at the real-estate office up to five days before she went into labor. When the time came, we rushed to the hospital, and

I went into the labor area with her and stayed until she was ready to deliver. Ed remained in the waiting room.

In the labor room, I was instructed to push on her back when the labor pains came. Then the nurse attached a mask containing a volatile anesthetic to Charmaine's wrist so she could sniff it when the labor pains came. When the pain started, Char would sniff the anesthetic and go into a light unconscious state for a few seconds and then her hand would drop, allowing her to breath air again, to regain consciousness. It worked at times during the ten hours she was in labor but wasn't too effective. The nurses came in to monitor her progress by measuring the descent of the head of our baby and a vaginal examination of cervical dilatation every few hours.

Back in 1956, the husbands weren't allowed in the delivery suite, so I had to sit outside the door and wait. After thirty minutes, a nurse came out smiling and said, "You have a big baby, but didn't tell if we had a boy or girl. Minutes later another nurse came out and said the same thing, smiling.

What was going on? What did they mean 'big baby.' I got worried. Was something wrong? But they were smiling so nothing could be wrong. I learned that our baby was about 7 pounds. Big baby? They didn't know what a big baby was. At birth I weighed 12 pounds, Charmaine, 11 pounds and her brother, 12 pounds. The ladies in those days were giving birth to little turkeys.

A few minutes later they wheeled Charmaine out and I went to her and held her hand. She looked at me smiling, "We have a little girl." I kissed her as they moved us along into a nice room. After being situated, a nurse came in and put a heat lamp between Char's elevated legs. This was to increase healing of the incision Dr. Newton made. Minutes later, another nurse brought in our little girl wrapped up in a white blanket and handed her to Charmaine.

"Your little daughter," she said.

Charmaine held her with her little face exposed; we saw the most beautiful little thing that came out of my wife. I got the weirdest feeling, realizing that now I'm not only a husband, but a father. A new role, I never gave much thought to earlier, but it felt good. I couldn't believe I was holding a new member of our family. We gave her the name of Paula Marie—Paula from my mother's name Pauline, and Charmaine's mother Marie. A nurse showed Ed into our room and Char asked if he'd like to hold his niece. All smiles, he said to Paula Marie, "I'm your Uncle Ed."

A couple of days later Charmaine was discharged from the hospital and given all the paperwork and the name of a pediatrician. It took us weeks to get used to our new arrival with the feeding, diaper changes, and the many hours of interrupted sleep. Char couldn't breast feed because Paula didn't seem to get enough nourishment, and the pediatrician put her on powdered Similac. We had to sterilize all the glass baby bottles and prepare the formula and put them in the fridge. Before feeding, a soft rubber nipple (teat) protruding from a cap had to be screwed on top of the bottle. There were no disposable diapers, only cloth diapers, nor plastic baby bottles during that time. As the months went by our little pride and joy was taking shape. At three months she was able to sit up on the couch without falling over. One evening at our dinner table, Paula in her bassinette next to me, started repeating, "Dada, dada." Char and I looked at each other smiling and surprised. I was pleased but was hit with the realization that now I really was her dad.

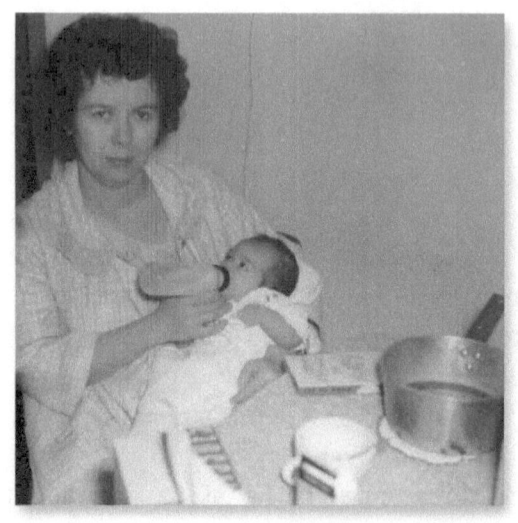

Charmaine with Paula

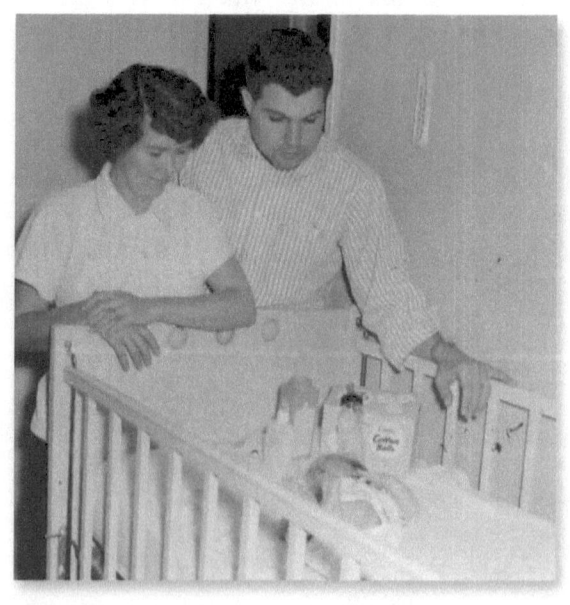

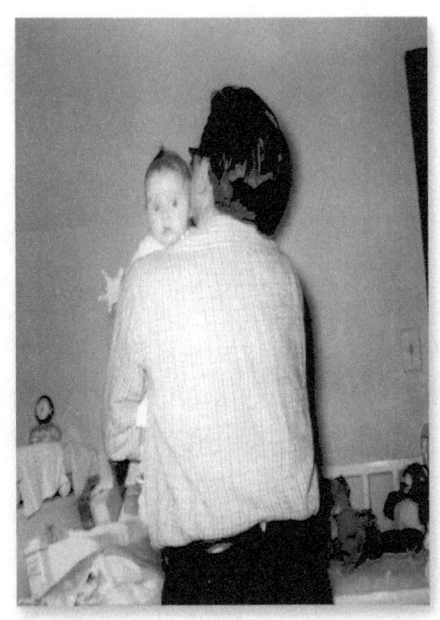

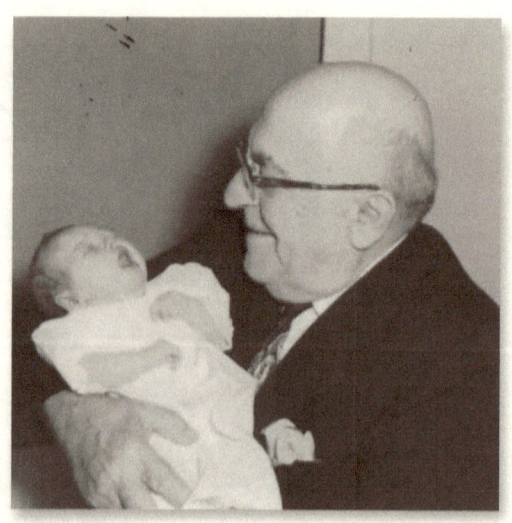

Bob's father with Paula

Ed with Paula

Bob's father and mother

CHAPTER 18
Oxford Bound to Attend Pharmacy School

In July of 1957, I received my letter from the Ole Miss Medical School admissions office. It was what I had been waiting for. Being a little anxious, I open it and learned that I was denied admission. They didn't give any reason. Charmaine and I were disappointed because we were told if we became residents I would be accepted. She could see the disappointment in my face. She was always there for me, and we talked about our future. Minutes later, I got a call from the Gross Anatomy Professor at the med school, who we were fortunate to know because he was Armenian, and my father being Armenian and an MD, we developed a very enjoyable relationship with him.

The professor wanted to know if I got my letter form Admissions. I felt he knew the outcome is why he called. He asked me if I were accepted. I said, "no." He asked me what I was going to do. I told him we now had a child, and I couldn't wait any longer, that Charmaine and I had talked about our future, and we decided we were going back to Oxford and enroll in Pharmacy School.

He said he was sorry I wasn't accepted and that he knew why and wanted to share it with me. He said I was first alternate, and they passed over me to take a student born and raised in Mississippi. I thanked him and told him how much we enjoyed visiting with him and that we would be fine.

In August we packed up and headed to Oxford. I had enrolled in

Pharmacy and Ed in the Chemistry Department, graduate program. majoring_in Biochemistry, with the assistance from the Admissions Office on the Oxford campus. When I told them I was a graduate, they said all I had to do was appear on a certain date for registration in the School of Pharmacy, that they would send over my name. They also registered Ed in the Chemistry Department. I then applied for housing.

The Chemistry Building was on the corner across from the Lyceum Building, which housed the administration offices—The Chancellor, vice-Chancellor and all the staff. Chemistry had three floors, and in 1957 the top floor was the Pharmacy School. It had a large classroom, four laboratories, a couple of faculty offices and the Dean's office. Some courses like anatomy/physiology and pharmacology were taught in the biology building, two buildings down from Chemistry on the south side of the circle.

This time we moved into a single-story two-bedroom apartment that was attached to three other units, unlike the two-story barrack-type building we lived in for my BA degree. There was a large parking area next to our building where we could see our car from the kitchen window. Paula slept in a room with us in a baby bed and Ed had the second room.

In February 1958, we learned during Char's visit to the doctor that she was pregnant with our second child, who was due around October 27th. That would make our second child appearing 25 months after Paula.

I was enjoying Pharmacy School immensely. Appreciated the courses and had some great teachers. Of all the courses, I felt an attraction to pharmaceutical chemistry—the chemistry of drugs.

Even though Charmaine and I saved money from working in Jackson, I felt the need to provide more income. Dr. Lewis Nobles, one of the best teachers I ever had anywhere, took me under his wing and gave me a job working in his undergraduate pharmacy lab preparing various solutions before his next lab, and keeping the storage room clean and in order.

I was enjoying pharmacy and all the science courses, especially anatomy and physiology, and pharmacology. The labs were helpful, and we operated on a dog to learn about the sympathetic and parasympathetic nervous systems.

In pharmacognosy we learned about medicinal drugs obtained from plants and other natural sources. They were called natural products. I collected a lot of samples and assembled my own home lab of natural products in glass jars. We had to learn the genus and species of hundreds of plants and during lab tests identify the plants. I remember Professor Johnson played a trick on us and placed a coffee bean on a plate that we were supposed to identify as we passed from one test sample to the next. No one got it. I thought it was a seed from a plant, but I missed it. He got a kick out of no one identifying the coffee bean.

During my second year I was awarded the Rexall Trophy from the Rexall Drug Company for outstanding achievement. And in my last year I was awarded the Taylor Medal in Pharmacy, the highest honor awarded to a student by the University of Mississippi.

Ed, Bob and Dr. Alton Bryant

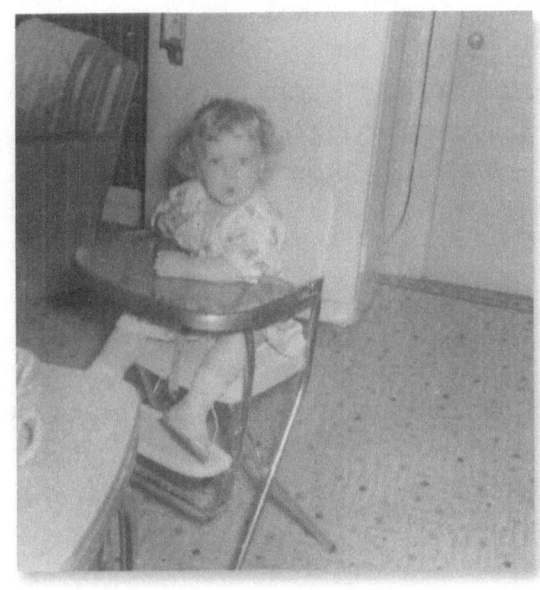

CHAPTER 19
Brother Ed in Love

My brother, Ed, and I were barbecuing in front of our apartment unit this one unseasonably warm evening in early spring 1958. I could tell something was bothering him, and I said, "What's up, brother?" He looked in deep thought about something.

He asked me if I would do him a favor.

"What's that?" I asked.

He hesitated, then asked me if I would call Hydig (hayrik is father in Armenian, but we pronounced it Hydig, when we were kids, and it stuck) about marrying Sandy Maksudian.

I said, "Sandy? You mean that little girl I used to see riding her tricycle up and down the sidewalk in front of her house?"

He nodded and said, "Yes."

I asked, "How old is she?"

"Sixteen."

"Sixteen! Are you c-r-a-z-y?"

He said, "Please. We have been dating the last few times I went home. We love each other. I need for you to call Hydig and asked him to convince the Maksudians to let Sandy marry me and that we love each other."

I said, "You're really serious?"

He nodded, "Yes, I can't concentrate on my studies. I want to marry Sandy. Hydig will listen to you."

I don't know where he got that idea. But I could see Ed was in pain. The love bug got him.

"Okay, I'll do it, but we'll go and make the call after dinner."

He agreed. "Thank you, thank you."

"You aren't going to kiss me, are you?" I said jokingly.

"I will if you'll do this for me."

"I was only joking. I can see you are serious."

He nodded as he turned the barbecue.

We told Charmaine everything, and in her sweet smiling way, thought it was so sweet and so nice.

I thought, *Am I the only sane one here?*

Then I remembered that Char and I started going together when she was sixteen, but we never thought about marriage then.

Around seven o'clock, Ed and I left in our Chevy and went to town, one block north of the square on Lamar to a phone booth that stood by the curb near a Kroger store. We couldn't afford a house phone. Ed and I squeezed into the phone booth, and I dropped coins in and dialed our folks' number. Mom answered and I asked to talk to Hydig.

"Is everything okay?" she asked,

"Yes, just want to ask him something. We are fine." Under my breath, I said, "*All except Ed.*"

When he came to the phone, I didn't know where to start. I just said, "Hydig, we have a little problem here."

"What's the problem?" he asked.

I said, "Ed has been dating Sandy Maksudian and is in love with her, and he wants you and mom to talk to Lolly and Arnold to convince them to allow Sandy to marry him. He said he's gonna fail in his courses. He can't study and can't get Sandy out of his mind."

Silence.

I wondered how he was going to respond to Ed's request. Instead, he laughed. "He's that bad?"

I said, "Yes. Do you think you and mom can convince them?"

He became silent again for a moment. I heard mom in the background asking, "What's wrong?"

Hydig said to her, "Nothing. I'll tell you when we hang up."

"So, what do you think?" I asked.

"We'll be in touch after we meet with them."

"Okay," I said and hung up.

"What did he say?" Ed asked. "C'mon, don't hold back."

I deliberately hesitated to make Ed sweat a little.

"Hydig said they would do it and he'll get back with us."

I never saw him happier. "Oh, I hope they agree." At this point when we left the phone booth, I kinda felt sorry for my brother. I knew how much I loved Charmaine. I was away from her for 20 months in the Army and didn't want to be away from her again.

Before a decision was made with the Maksudians, we got word that Lolly, Sandy's mother, wanted to come visit us. Ed, Char, Paula, and I piled into our Chevy and drove to the Memphis airport, 90 miles from Oxford, to get Lolly. I met her at the gate and grabbed her luggage and led the way to the car that Ed was driving around until he saw us standing at the curb. When he stopped, I opened the back door for Lolly, and she slid in next to Paula and Charmaine. I threw her luggage in the trunk and slid into the driver's side and Ed moved to the passenger side after greeting his future mother-in-law. Immediately she took to our little two-year old blonde daughter, Paula, who seemed attracted to Lolly, too. Lolly asked to hold Paula in her lap.

We knew she came to check out our living conditions on campus and to look over Oxford. I knew once Lolly saw how Charmaine survived as a student's wife, and with a child, she would realize Charmaine could be a good companion for Sandy. She stayed two days, and we took her all over town and out to eat. Apparently, we passed the test because Ed and Sandy made plans to get married the next year in June 1959.

CHAPTER 20
Birth of Our Second Child: Cindy Lyn

Around five pm this Monday evening of October 27, 1958, Charmaine went into labor with our second child. I hurried to the phone booth and called her ob-gyn doctor. No answer. I called the hospital where he was on staff, and they said he was detained in Memphis. My mind went blank. Now I was scared. They didn't recommend any other doctor. *What?!!! What was going on?* I didn't want to just take her to the hospital. I wanted a doctor I knew.

I thought about the town of Jericho in Scripture, my wall was falling but there was a beacon of hope for those who trusted in the Lord. Why I thought of that, I don't know. Hope was what I was after. I felt desperate and alone. I told myself to calm down. Once I did, I thought about Dr. James Gilmore, our family doctor. I called and was able to reach him and told him our predicament. I could hear him breathing in the phone.

"Please Dr. Gilmore," I said under my breath.

"I'll be glad to, Bob," he said. "I'll meet you at the hospital."

I sighed in relief. I thanked him at least three times and rushed back to our apartment and immediately helped Charmaine into the car and drove her to the Oxford Hospital. My brother Ed was there to watch after Paula, our two-year-old.

When we got to the Oxford Hospital, the nurse looked at me with a strange expression. I told her the story about Char's ob-gyn doctor and that Dr. Gilmore was going to deliver our baby. She took Charmaine down the hall to the back and into a room, which I figured was the delivery room. I sat in the waiting room where I could see down the hall.

Minutes later Dr. Gilmore came in through a side door and entered the delivery room. A little over an hour had passed and I saw the nurse and orderly wheel Charmaine into a room across from the delivery room. I looked at my watch and it was a little after 7:00 pm. Minutes later the nurse came out of the room and walked towards me.

"Your wife's doing fine." She said, "Time for you to go in to see her and your daughter."

A daughter? Wow. Another girl.

I followed the nurse into the room and went to the beside and bent down to kiss Charmaine, who was still in a daze, but alert enough.

"We have another daughter," she was able to say.

"Yes. I know. The nurse just told me."

"Are you happy with another girl?"

"Of course. All I care about is that she's healthy. And the nurse assured me she was."

There was a knock on the door. The nurse entered and said, "Here's your daughter." She moved in toward us and placed Cindy Lyn in Charmaine's arms. I chose the name Cindy when we were thinking about names because I liked the song Cindy. Char opened the blanket around Cindy's face. She was so pretty.

"Hold your daughter," she said.

I took her into my arms and looked into her dark eyes and kissed her on the forehead.

"This child is on the darker side," I said to Charmaine.

"That's the Armenian side of the Magarians," she said.

Charmaine noticed that Cindy had dark hair down the sides of her face, like sideburns, down her arms, and body too, and it kind of worried her. She asked the nurse if the hair was permanent.

"Oh, honey," the nurse said with a little laugh. "It will all be gone in a few days."

I couldn't help from laughing. *Our little monkey.*

I stepped out into the hall to go to the men's room and met the nurse that first took Charmaine into the delivery room. She smiled at me and said I was supposed to take my wife to the Bramlett Hospital. Both hospitals were small, and Dr. Gilmore was on staff there and not at the Oxford hospital.

He and the nurse were so kind; they didn't make a big deal of it. I figured they knew I was shaken. But, in my defense, her ob-gyn doctor never told us we had to take Charmaine to the Bramlett hospital and that he was on staff there. I learned in confidence from that nurse that he had a drinking problem and was sleeping it off in Memphis.

Two days later, back home with our new baby, it was time for me to go see Dr. Gilmore to pay our bill for delivering Cindy. I had checked and the going rate for delivery was $150. We had no insurance. I was praying it wasn't more. I went to the Bramlett clinic which was in a two-story white house on North Lamar and reported in to see Dr. Gilmore. Didn't need an appointment. Moments later, he came out of his office and waved me in.

I sat in a chair by his desk facing him. He asked how Charmaine and the baby were doing.

"Fine, sir. Charmaine wanted me to make sure I told you how much we appreciated you for delivering our daughter, Cindy."

"Oh, happy to do it. Cindy eating a lot?"

I nodded and said, "And sleeping a lot?"

He smiled.

"I've come to pay our bill. How much do we owe you, Dr. Gilmore?"

He looked at me and frowned. A few seconds later, he said, "Oh, Bob, you're still in pharmacy school."

"But we owe you, sir."

He smiled. "Would $50 be okay?"

I was shocked, and asked, "Are you sure?"

He raised his hands. "Sure. That'll be fine."

I stood up and thanked him, shaking his hand. I felt like hugging him.

"You don't know how much we appreciate you, Dr. Gilmore."

"Remember. I was a student once and know how it is with a family."

When I left his office, I went to the nurses' station and told them what Dr. Gilmore said I owed.

When I arrived at home and told Charmane what he charged, she too, was surprised and thankful. We didn't have much money at the time and were equally pleased when the Oxford Hospital bill was only $100. I can't remember if we sent Dr. Gilmore a thank-you card, but it would be something we'd do. I thought to myself, *I wish there were more doctors like Dr. Gilmore.*

While pursuing my studies in pharmacy, I learned about a professional fraternity in early Fall of 1958, the Kappa Psi Pharmaceutical Fraternity. One of the members invited me to one of their "Smokers." During that time, a smoker was just as the name implies—where everyone gathered to learn about the Fraternity and during that time you were free to smoke. Packs of cigarettes were opened on a table, but I didn't join in because I had quit when I came back from Korea.

During the meeting, I looked around at the members. Their professional demeanor, and friendliness impressed me. Dressed in suits and ties, they looked the part of a pharmacist. The president opened the meeting with a welcome, then presented an interesting summary of the goals of the Fraternity and how the Beta Rho Chapter of Kappa Psi fitted into the plan. When finished, he introduced Dr. Nobles, their faculty advisor (had the title of GCD—Grand Council Deputy), who spoke movingly about his experiences in the Fraternity. He was an initiate of Beta Rho. Next, Dr. Elmer Hammond, dean of the College of Pharmacy, spoke about his initiation at the University of Wisconsin. He was a tall man who spoke very keenly about what Kappa Psi meant to him, followed by Dr. Austin Dodge, and initiate of Eta Chapter at the Philadelphia College of Pharmacy. He took more time to tell us about his experiences. Dr. Dodge was known for his long-winded conversations and lectures, but I found him to be a good instructor in Pharmaceutical Chemistry. After the meeting, I thought about all the speeches, and I became excited to join Beta Rho. I was initiated in the fall of 1958.

Since Charmaine and I now had two children—Paula Marie and Cindy Lyn—I was searching for ways to add to our savings that we earned in Jackson. Now, Charmaine was busy taking care of the little ones while I was concentrating on my studies. I made sure I found time to help her, but she was an exceptional mother, always smiling, patient, and loved attending to the girls. Motherhood really agreed with her. I was proud of her. I figured her motherly instincts had kicked in.

A few months after my initiation into Beta Rho, I learned that Dr. Nobles was working with a Survey Company out east that was interested in accumulating data on the drugs doctors were prescribing across the nation. Knowing that I needed work, he offered me the position of supervising a team of four Beta Rho brothers to copy drug names from doctors' prescriptions onto computer cards. Once a month on different Sundays we'd enter the four pharmacies in Oxford, the one pharmacy in Pontotoc, the one in Tupelo, and the one in Grenada. A couple of the stores did 500 scripts a day, which was a WOW during that era. The Company not only paid us per computer card, but also paid for my gas mileage, which helped. While it took half a day for us to copy the drug names onto computer cards, we enjoyed the task because we learned the names and dosages of each drug from copying them so often. I learned much, which helped me in my classes since I never worked a day in a pharmacy.

During my senior year in '59, I earned additional income working at Peel Drugs in Holy Springs, 20 miles north of Oxford. Besides learning a lot in the pharmacy from Billy Peel, the owner, I enjoyed working with the farmers, learning the meds and injections they used for their cattle. Mr. Peel asked me if I would be interested in working with him after graduation. I appreciated the offer, but I wasn't interested in working full time in Holly Springs.

That summer after their June wedding and their honeymoon, Ed and Sandy moved to Oxford. They rented one of the units close to us. Sandy and Charmaine became close friends and Sandy seemed to take to her new environment. They were good for each other. We enjoyed being together and especially glad to be there for her. Sandy enrolled in her senior year in Oxford High School, which was at the east edge of campus, and after graduation she worked in the Ole Miss athletic department.

Before I was graduated from the School of Pharmacy, Dr. Nobles asked me to stay on as his graduate student in pharmaceutical chemistry.

I told him I'd love to, but we had bills with Penny's and Sears, buying clothes and items for the girls, and I needed to work to pay them off. He understood, but said if I ever wanted to return, he'd be happy to have me as one of his graduate students.

During my last semester, Charmaine and I and the girls went for an interview at Stiehl Drugs in Collinsville, Illinois for a pharmacist position. The offer included a big perk: living in a one-story, two-bedroom brick house rent free that was attached to the Stiehl Drugs building. I would only have to walk out the door, turn right and walk four feet to the door that led directly into the prescription area of the store. I wouldn't have to spend money for gas, which was a big savings for us just getting started. They offered me the position with the house and a salary I was pleased to accept.

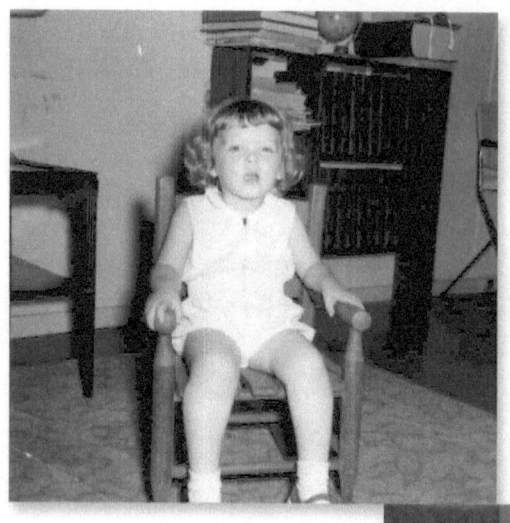

*Bob & Charmaine's second
child, Cindy*

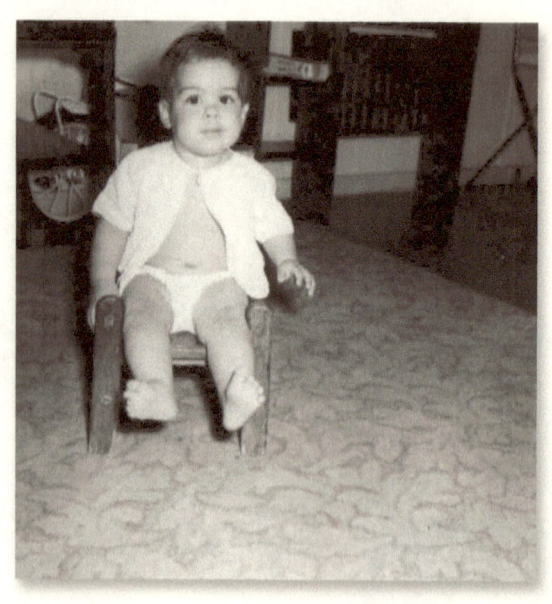

CHAPTER 21
Bound for Stiehl Drugs: Collinsville, Illinois

After finishing Pharmacy School in January 1960, we packed up and moved to Collinsville. The Stiehl family owned four pharmacies, our store and the one in downtown Collinsville, and two in other cities. The main store was in Belleville, Illinois.

Our store was located on the west side of town. Agnus and Laverne were the two ladies who worked the front end of our store. Laverne was a fantastic person, easy to work with, always friendly to everyone. Agnus was somewhat reserved. She and I didn't hit it off too well at first. She tried twice to come behind the prescription counter to help me but got in my way. I told her to stay out in front where she belonged and that she didn't have the training to be with me. She thought because she helped the previous pharmacist, who was transferred downtown, that I, too, would like her help. No way. It didn't take long for me to learn that there were a few things that went on in the pharmacy that didn't suit me, and I stopped them. I refused on several occasions to dispense drugs that were not covered by doctor's prescriptions. Agnus called the main office in Belleville and told management that I wasn't filing some prescriptions. To my surprise, one of the supervisors I knew appeared at our store and told me about the call from Agnus and what she had said. I explained to him about the unethical practices that were going on in the pharmacy before I arrived, and I had stopped them. I told him if the Illinois State Board of Pharmacy found out about it, everyone in the pharmacy could lose their license, and the store put on probation, and I couldn't be part of it, and hoped he understood.

I could tell from his facial expressions that he was upset to hear the details. He apologized about Agnus and said he'd handle it, but more importantly, he was pleased to know what was going on in the pharmacy and that I was not part of it. Agnus never again stepped behind the prescription counter and kept her distance from me. I later surmised that management knew more about Agnus' behavior than I realized.

A new manager was hired. Roy was older, probable in his early fifties, and I was thirty. He was easy to work with, but somewhat set in his ways and too business-like with the customers, which didn't set well with them nor with me. He also was big on cutting cost on everything, even when ordering drugs from the wholesaler: purchasing generics and dispensing them when the doctors were prescribing meds from the original manufacturer. I didn't like it, nor did I dispense them.

I know this sounds like I was arrogant and a person with whom others couldn't get along. It wasn't that, I just wanted to be ethical and follow good practices. After a month in the pharmacy, we learned that Charmaine was pregnant with our third child. I told her we had to stop moving because every time we did, she got pregnant. You'd think by then, we'd know how babies were formed.

During the sunny spring days, Charmaine would walk our girls—Paula, now 4, and Cindy now 2—to the corner of the store, which was only fifteen feet from our door, allowing the girls to continue around the corner to the store front. Paula would open the door, and they'd enter on their own while Charmaine watched at a distance. Standing on the platform behind the prescription counter, I could see the entire store—who came in and who went out. The girls would come in holding hands and as they got a few feet into the store they would look at me and smile, Cindy with her big brown eyes and Paula with a smile that said, "*Look at us, dad.*" Every time they came in Laverne would always rush to the cash register to meet them.

Paula would ask, "Lady, do you have any candy?"

Laverne would say, "Sure do, girls," and gave them each two or three pieces to outstretched little hands. They had no money and didn't pay, but dad took care of that.

They'd turn and start retracing their steps heading out, but when they got midway, they'd always make sure to look at dad with a smile that said: "*Look what we got, dad.*" I had the urge to run out from behind the counter and grab them and kiss them. I waited until I got home to do that.

Senator Estes Kefauver, D-Tenn., came to St. Louis to lead a significant congressional inquiry into the rising drug costs and drug-company profits. Unfortunately, it incited many of our patients, who harassed Roy and me while waiting for us to fill their scripts. They took every opportunity to annoy us with questions as:

"You making 300% on your meds today? You pharmacists still screwing the public?"

Unfortunately, they didn't listen to the full Kefauver report, which determined that the drug companies were being investigated for the rising costs and profits, not us. I got tired of hearing their complaints and was glad when the committee finished and left town.

We had patients that had many prescriptions on file with us, which were refilled often. Many of whom had charge accounts with us, something that was common during that time. Ninety-nine percent of them were very good about paying their bills. I got to know an elderly couple, the Martins, who were among our best customers. Mr. Martin and I became friends through our many conversations while he was waiting to have his scripts filled. He was quite the outdoorsman, and once told me how large the blue gill were where he went fishing. While I wasn't much of a fisherman, I liked the idea of being in a boat on a lake early in the morning. Seemed like it would be very relaxing. Once when he came in, I asked if he would like a fishing buddy. He said he'd love it. His old fishing buddy had moved away.

It got to the point where I had to spend a day away from the pharmacy. Mr. Martin and I would go fishing. We would be on the water in Red Bud, Illinois, 32 miles south of Collinsville, by 5 a.m., sitting in a rowboat filled with our equipment, lunches, and coolers filled with water and soft drinks. Around 2:00 p. m. we'd call it a day and head back to shore, pack up and go into town, and stop off at the local tavern to have a cold beer. I'd get home around five after dropping off Mr. Martin at his home. I loved it.

In December I asked Roy about giving Mr. Martin a carton of Camel cigarettes for Christmas because he spends a lot of money with us, and besides it would be good for business. Well, you'd have thought the roof was falling in. He said with scorn, "That's crazy. Were in the business to make money, not give it away."

I didn't respond. I knew it wouldn't do any good.

A week before Christmas, I opened the store and Roy didn't come in until twelve noon. The pharmacist who opens the store got off at five p.m. and the one who came in at noon closed the store at nine p.m. I knew Mr. Martin was coming in before noon because he called me with his prescription numbers. He and I talked about fishing and a lot about his family each time he came in. This day, while Laverne and Agnus were busy with customers, I went to the register and reached below for a carton of Camel cigarettes, took it to the prescription counter and wrapped it in Christmas paper. Then I took it to the register and placed it on the shelf underneath. I rang it up on the register and paid for it out of my own pocket. Then I went to the card rack in front of the store to get a Christmas card, addressed it to Mr. Martin, and wrote inside the card how much we appreciated his business and thanked him for being a loyal customer. Then I placed it under the carton of cigarettes.

Later that morning, Mr. Martin pulled into the parking lot. I had his prescriptions filled and was waiting for him. He moseyed over to the prescription area where we talked a little and then we went to the register for him to pay for his meds. I immediately said, "Mr. Martin. I have something for you." I reached underneath the register and pulled out the carton of cigarettes and card and handed it to him.

He frowned. "What's this?"

"Oh, nothing much, just a little token to show our appreciation for your business with us. You and Mrs. Martin have been with us a long time and we really do appreciate it."

He opened the card and read my words. He looked up at me. "You didn't have to do this," he said with tears in his eyes. "Cigarettes?"

"Yes, sir."

You'd have thought I gave him a thousand dollars. He was so

thankful, I thought he was going to cry. He shook his head, "Don't get much in the way of presents these days. You know, we old folks are almost forgotten."

"Aw, no. You and I are fishing buddies. I'd never forget you, Mr. Martin," I said with a tightness in my throat. "We at Stiehl's appreciate you."

He quickly turned and raised the cartoon in the air to thank me as he left so not to show how emotional he was.

Bob in Prescription Area

Gray Burcham

CHAPTER 22
The Birth of Our Third Child: Leslie Ann

In November 1960, Leslie, our third daughter was born, but came in an emergency. I had just walked into the kitchen from the pharmacy for lunch and Char was on the phone with Little Teckla, our cousin. She and Char were talking away, and I hadn't been in the kitchen five minutes when suddenly a gush of blood flooded down Char's legs and into her shoes. I grabbed the phone, hung it up, quickly carried her into the bedroom, raised her feet up on pillows and put a pillow between her legs. We were facing placenta previa—placenta being close to the cervix, and it had detached. Scared, I quickly called Laverne, who worked the front end of the pharmacy. She came running in and told me to call the ambulance and she'd stay with the girls.

No 911 then. The ambulance came in seconds and worked on Char for a few minutes, then rushed her into the ambulance, and they raced down Collinsville Road to East St. Louis and pulled into Christian Welfare Hospital. I had a devil of a time trying to keep up with their strobes flashing and sirens blasting. When I got to the ER, Char was taken somewhere. I wasn't told where. I presumed to the OR. As always, they tell you to go to the waiting room and that someone would keep me informed. I asked if they were going to call her specialist, Dr. Semen (funny name for an ob-gyn specialist). They told me they'd handle it. I went to the waiting room in a daze worried about Char and the baby, I called my mother, and she called my dad, who was in

102

his office. They let me sit there for such a long time with all sorts of fearful thoughts. An hour had passed, and no one came to me. I was going out of my mind.

What in the world was going on? Was anyone ever going to tell me? So many bad things were going through my mind. Is Charmaine okay and the baby? Oh, God, please let them be okay.

My mother got a message to me through one of the nurses, and I called her. She told me my dad was coming to the hospital. When they came for me, Char had just arrived in a room. She was still unconscious. I learned both mother and daughter were fine.

Thank you, Lord! Thank you! I sighed a huge relief!

My dad came to the room to tell us everything was okay. We hugged and I thanked him for coming. Later I learned my dad came to the OR and a nurse called out to him, "Sir, you can't go in there." The other nurse told her, "That's Dr. Magarian, he can go anywhere he wants."

Dr. Semen had to do a C-Section and flip Char to drain the blood. I learned later that my dad gave him a kiss on his check—good ole Armenian custom—when they met up in the OR. Dr. Semen and my dad were the best of friends, and he came to my dad's office on scheduled visits to spend a day examining the women that my dad recommended to see him. The ladies were African American, and many wouldn't go downtown to the doctors' offices.

After several days Char was released from the hospital with our little girl, Leslie Ann. We now had three daughters. Paula, 4 years old, Cindy 2, and Leslie, our new bambina, born November 14, 1960.

CHAPTER 23
Experiences in the Pharmacy Setting

Early in the spring of '61 a young couple came into the pharmacy, and I waited on them and learned from the husband that he was an engineer and worked in St. Louis at the Arch. His wife was a homebody with three children and was very friendly, I asked if they'd like to come over some time and meet my wife and maybe have a cookout. They thought it was a wonderful idea. That evening, I told Charmaine about them, and she was pleased to have an opportunity to meet the couple. I invited them over the following weekend for a cookout. That social event brought us closer together; she and Charmaine really got along well. We went to the movies in St. Louis a few times and the hockey games. During our association with them she started calling Charmaine "Char" for short, and asked if that was okay. We liked it and it took hold. Besides this couple we also had very enjoyable times with Charmaine's sister Jeanie and her husband Tony Ortiz.

As the months passed, I realized that the retail end of pharmacy wasn't for me. Since my undergraduate days, I had been interested in developing new drugs to treat breast cancer. In the spring of '61, I wrote Dr. Nobles and asked if the option of coming to Ole Miss as his graduate student in the Fall was still open. He was pleased to hear from me and told me yes, it was, and for me to apply for an AFPE (American Foundation for Pharmaceutical Education) fellowship. He wrote that since my grades were excellent and I had won several awards in Pharmacy, along with the Taylor Medal, the highest honor a student can receive at the University of Mississippi, that I would be a good candidate for the fellowship. It would pay for my tuition, books, and supplies. He would supplement it with a stipend.

Now, I knew I had to talk it over with Char hoping she would see what I saw for our future in pursuing the Ph.D. in Medicinal Chemistry. She had known of my keen interest in research, and this was a decision I felt good about, but wouldn't proceed without her blessings. We were faced with leaving a well-paid job, having three little girls and just learned she was pregnant again, and returning to Oxford for another several years. We had paid off our Pennys and Sears bills and had a nice savings. We had no debts. Char was so loving and kind, and in our biblical marriage, we always operated on the same wavelength.

After dinner that evening, when the children were asleep, we sat in the living room and had a conversation that would change our lives. I told her what I had done and explained at length my plan, and what our future could hold for us in teaching and research. We discussed every angle of what we'd be facing. We both felt working together we could do it only back in Oxford, our second home. She said she wanted to do what I wanted. I hugged her and gave her a kiss to remember.

I received notices that I was awarded the AFPE Fellowship and was accepted into the graduate program with Dr. Nobles as my major professor. I gave notice to Stiehl drugs that I'd be leaving as of July 01, 1961. My brother Ed was still at Ole Miss working on his Ph.D. in biochemistry, and with his help we were able to get an apartment in Vet's village beneath him and Sandy. We learned that all the old frame buildings were gone and replaced with new two-story brick buildings.

Charmaine's parents and my parents were pleased about our plan to work on the Ph.D., but many of our relatives thought we were crazy. One asked my dad if I were going to be a student for life. One thing about us, we didn't care what other people thought. Our life was between Charmaine and me. I was reminded of this middle-aged man that came into our pharmacy every several months just to get one tablet of prescribed phenobarbital. I never charged him. One night when he came in, he said, "I guess you've wondered why I come for my one tablet."

I hesitated but said, "Yes, I have."

He said he was an alcoholic, and whenever he felt like he was going to fall off the wagon, he'd come to the pharmacy to get the one tablet his doctor prescribed. The phenobarbital calmed him enough to fight off the temptation to have a drink. He went on to say that he always wanted to go to college but got married, bought a house, and had a mortgage. He never saw a way to accomplish his dream, and it drove him to drinking.

I asked him if he ever checked on the different options that maybe could help him reach his goal? He unfortunately had a defeatist attitude, and I thought about several suggestions but decided to let it drop because I was no psychologist, and I realized he no longer had a strong motivation to pursue higher education.

I always believed there was a way with God's help. One had to pray about it and when the feeling was right, go for it. We decided that if we went to graduate school and had a hard time, I could always go back to work as a pharmacist, since I was licensed in Illinois and Mississippi.

One warm day in June, a month before we left for Ole Miss, an interesting thing happened. I came out of the back door of the Pharmacy and was passing by our bedroom window to enter our home, when to my surprise, little Leslie in her baby bed close to the open, screened-in window, jumped up when she saw me and said, "Hi!" That really warmed my heart.

Cindy, Leslie & Paula

CHAPTER 24
Bound for Oxford: To Work on My Ph.D.

The day had arrived in July, '61 when the moving van loaded our furniture, and we watched as they took off. I had said my goodbyes to my friends in Stiehl's pharmacy and it was time that we loaded ourselves into our '54 Chevy with Charmaine's mother, Marie, and our three girls in the back seat, and pregnant Char up front with me. We drove off, heading south. I couldn't help but feel like the family in John Steinbeck's *The Grapes of Wrath*, heading south in our '54 Chevy, instead of heading west on route 66 to California as they did.

The apartment we moved into in Vet's Village was much nicer and more modern than the frame buildings we lived in four-and-a-half years earlier when I earned my BA degree.

Interestingly, my brother Ed was directing the movers into our downstairs two-bedroom apartment. We were able to stay in our new home that night. Two days later, I met with my advisor, Dr. Lewis Nobles, who became the graduate dean of the University of Mississippi and had his office on the second floor of the Chemistry Building. The building was a light brown three-story brick building with five concrete steps leading up to two tall heavy doors. The first floor had classrooms, a stock room and a large auditorium. The second floor had the Chemistry Department Chairman's office, a library, several labs, Dr. Nobles' large dean's office, and a couple of faculty offices. On the third floor was the Pharmacy School, which occupied the entire floor, consisting of the Dean's office, three laboratories, a dispensing laboratory, a large auditorium, a stock room, and a faculty office. A couple labs had an area in the back that faculty used as their offices.

In my meeting with Dr. Nobles, we discussed what curriculum I needed to follow to earn the Ph.D. Unfortunately, I would be required to take several undergraduate courses needed as prerequisites to enter graduate level courses, which meant an extra year. It appeared it would be four to five years for me. With my schedule in hand, I stopped at his secretary's desk to sign for my stipend.

My first year in Graduate School was a challenge. I had to enroll in the Chemistry Department since the Pharmacy medicinal chemistry Ph.D. program hadn't been approved yet. Also, I would have to enroll into the required undergraduate courses—two semesters of undergraduate Physical Chemistry, three semesters of Calculus, and one semester of Differential Equations—to proceed into some of the graduate courses. My graduate Organic Chemistry was a challenge, and it kept me up studying late at night since I had my undergraduate courses nine years earlier. I had to review my undergraduate textbook and seek the help of Ed, who was sharp in chemistry.

Normally, graduate students are assigned an office but there were no vacant rooms in the Chemistry Department, so I spent my days in the chemistry library for the first semester. In the second semester, Dr. Nobles found us offices on the second floor in the Lyceum building. Ed shared the room with me. Above us on the third floor were a couple of students in Pharmacy Administration. One of the students became very prominent in later years. His name was Mickey Smith, whom I got to know very well during our graduate years. His hometown was in Missouri near St. Louis, my home area, and a graduate of the St. Louis College of Pharmacy.

Dr. John McLaurin, an ob-gyn specialist, was recommended to us since Char would have another C-section. The walls of the uterus became thinner after her first C-section with Leslie, and the doctor didn't want to chance a normal delivery. He recommended tying her fallopian tubes during the surgery because he knew she didn't want to undergo another C-section. Neither did I.

In my second year in the graduate program, the Pharmacy Medicinal

Chemistry Ph.D. program was approved, and I was transferred out of the chemistry department into the College of Pharmacy graduate program.

Ed was doing well in graduate Biochemistry but became interested in my program of drug discovery and decided he wanted in the same Ph.D. program with Dr. Nobles, so he transferred in with Nobles' approval.

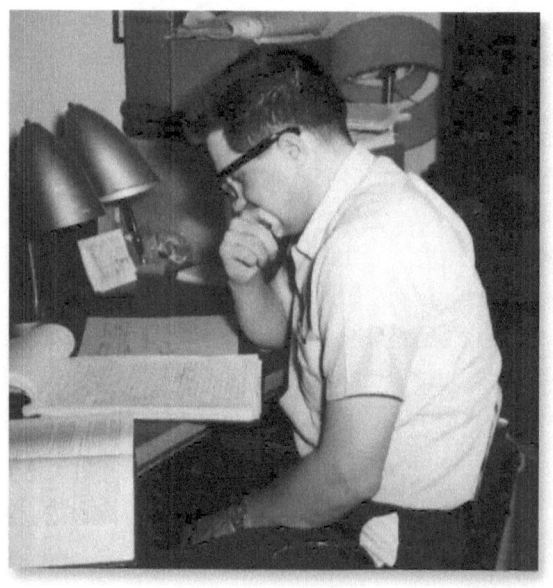

CHAPTER 25
Birth Of Our Fourth Child: Robert Dwight

A lot was happening in 1962.

The summer of that year was Charmaine's time to have our fourth child. The doctor set the date of July 6 for her C-section. That morning, I took her to the Oxford hospital, where she was admitted, and I was allowed to spend time with her in the room while they prepped her. We had wondered if we were getting a boy this time. When the nurses came for her, I went to the waiting room and sat where I could see down the hall again. After about thirty minutes, a nurse came out of the OR and gave me a thumbs up to indicate that we had a boy. An hour later I saw them moving Charmaine into a room across from the delivery room. A few minutes later, a nurse came out and waved for me to come to her. She said I could go in. Charmaine was sitting up with a few pillows behind her but looked a little dazed.

"We have our boy," I told her.

She nodded. "I heard them talking before they brought me out."

There was a knock on the door and in came a nurse with our son bundled up in a warm blanket and handed him to his mother. I eagerly waited to see his face. He had a round red face. I kissed him on his head and his eyes opened. "Hello, Robert D.," I said. We earlier decided on Robert D. and would call him Bobby D. While still admiring our little boy, a nurse knocked on the open door and told us that William Faulkner had died. This was a date we wouldn't forget, since it was the same day as the birth of our son.

Dorothy Kelly becomes our maid in 1962.

Two months after we brought Bobby home, we were looking for a maid to take care of the children while Charmaine went back to work. We traded at the Tidwell's grocery and service station down on the highway near the campus. We asked her if she knew of anyone. She recommended Dorothy, a middle-aged black woman who came to our apartment to interview for the maid's position. Dorothy was very nice but a little quiet. Back then, maids charged very reasonable rates. We came to an agreement on what she wanted, and she started the next day. Charmaine worked with her for a couple of months and learned that Dorothy had a routine that was very effective in housecleaning and taking care of our children. Paula was 6 and in the first grade, Cindy was 4, Leslie was 2, and Bobby, our newborn.

After Char was confident in Dorothy, she took a job as secretary to Mr. William S. Griffin, Director of Alumni Activities. She worked for him for one year and then became secretary to the Assistant Dean of Engineering, Dr. Frank A. Anderson, who was a jewel of a man.

It was a blessing to have Dorothy help Char because my day consisted of classes, working in the lab every chance I got, and studying at night at the kitchen table in the wee hours of the morning. This continued until I earned my Ph.D. But to get it I also had to select my Ph.D. Dissertation Committee members, which consisted of Dr. Lewis Nobles as chair, Dr. Joseph Sam, Chair of the Medicinal Chemistry Department, Dr. Norman Dorenbos, faculty member, and Dr. William Nes, faculty member in the Chemistry Department. During my first meeting with the committee, I presented my research project that Dr. Nobles and I selected and sought their approval of my dissertation work to proceed.

One advantage of working for the university is that Char could put our name on the list for Staff Housing. The university had frame homes on the edge of the campus that staff could rent. It wasn't long after she signed up, we were able to move into a two-story white frame house. We occupied the 3-bedroom lower level, and another couple were on the second floor.

Our children really took to Dorothy, and she was excellent. She even cooked for us. One morning Char put a package of hamburger meat on the table and when Dorothy came, she asked Dorothy if she would make us a meatloaf. Dorothy didn't say a word, and according to her body language, we didn't think she would. But when we came home that evening after work, she had the meatloaf made and on the stove. It was great. She was a great cook.

The next time Char wanted her to make us a meatloaf, she told me to ask Dorothy. Char didn't think she liked the wife asking her. This was very perceptive of Char. I asked Dorothy and she said, "Yes, Mr. Robert," with a smile. We learned later that in the current southern culture, the maids liked the man of the house to give them orders. At noon, when we came home for lunch, we'd watch an episode of *As the World Turns* after eating. One day, Dorothy was standing in the kitchen doorway watching with us. I told her to come and sit with us to enjoy the 30-minute program. She wouldn't.

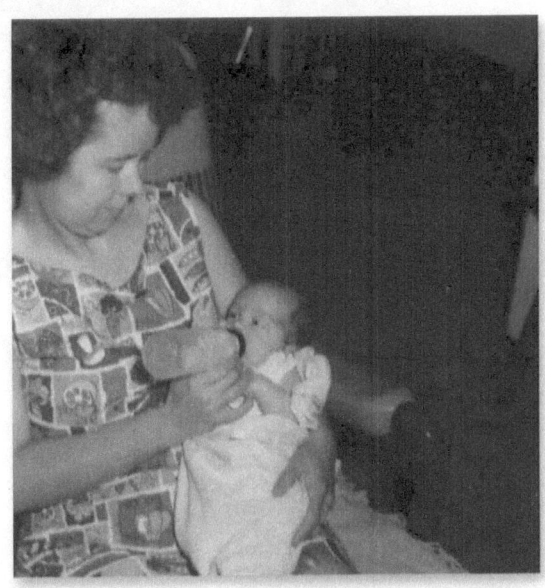

CHAPTER 26
James Meredith Integrates Ole Miss

In late September, I drove down Fraternity Row to the highway to Tidwell's Service Station where we bought groceries. This day the highway patrol had a car parked across the road blocking anyone from coming on campus, at the point where the campus road ended at the highway. The patrolmen waved at me to stop. He asked me where I was going. Once I told him he said for me to hurry back and stay on campus.

"What's going on?" I asked. He wouldn't say. Later, driving around the campus I saw highway patrol cars blocking all roads leading into the university. I realized that maybe the rumors were true. Someone was going to try and integrate our university. The next afternoon I drove around campus and saw a commotion with police cars at the bridge leading out on University Avenue heading towards town. I parked and got out of my car and walked over and stood by the curb in front of the Catholic Church and watched as several State Police cars were bunched together, blocking the entrance to the campus. To my surprise, there, standing next to a black sedan, was Governor Ross Barnett. He was only five feet from me. I recognized him because he used to come into the Emporium in Jackson and shake my hand and ask for my vote. He was running for governor then. Now, I knew why he was there—to block the entrance of the person who was coming. I looked to my left and coming toward campus were two black vehicles moving toward us in the center of the road, single file, and finally stopping withing ten feet of the Governor. The back door of the first vehicle opened onto the inside of the street and a marshal dressed in a black suit and tie helped a young black man dressed in a suit out of the vehicle. They walked together over to the governor.

The marshal said, "Governor Barnett, we are here to enroll Mr. James Meredith in the University of Mississippi."

The Governor said, "Sir, I cannot allow that to happen."

The marshal said, "Sir, what you are saying is that you will not allow Mr. Meredith to enroll in the University of Mississippi?"

"Yes, sir. That's what I'm saying."

The marshal guided James Meredith back to the first vehicle and they entered it. Both vehicles turned around and headed back to town, presumable back to Memphis.

Everyone dispersed after the marshals left, but the State Patrol officers remained blocking the entrance.

We had been watching the news every night since then. The university set up telephone booths in front of the Lyceum building for the press, and there were a lot of 'em there. Either on Saturday September 29th or Sunday September 30th, President John F. Kennedy was on TV asking for the cooperation of the good people of Mississippi to allow Mr. Meredith to enroll in their university.

On Sunday afternoon, September 30th, I had just come out of the Chemistry Building where I was doing some literature research and was walking to the corner close to the Lyceum building when I heard a roaring noise. To my surprise, a few two-and-a- half- ton Army trucks came racing onto campus and stopped in front of the Lyceum building. I remembered those trucks from my time in the Army in Korea. Marshals wearing protective body and head gear and carrying weapons jumped out of the back and surrounded the building, standing shoulder-to-shoulder. I saw a group of unsavory-looking individuals rushing through the streets heading towards the marshals and I immediately took off for home and turned on the TV. The Highway Commissioner came on and stated that he pulled the patrol cars off the entrances to the campus. "If the government wants to take over, then they can do it," he said. A riot began.

We wondered through the night what was happening. On Monday morning, October first, I went on campus, and it looked like a war zone. The rioters were nowhere in sight, only some marshals and the press. The streets surrounding the Lyceum Building were filled with fragments of bricks. Close to the east entrance of the campus, a science building named Hume Hall was under construction and there were stacks of bricks outside the building. These were the bricks the rioters gathered to throw at the marshals. At that brick site, a boy from Water Valley was shot and killed, most likely from a stray bullet because it was a good distance from the marshals. Don't remember any more deaths.

Of course, most classes were canceled, and the campus was literally shut down. I understand that Pharmacy classes were in session until the Dean cancelled them because of the choking fumes from the remnants of tear gas. On Tuesday October 2, 1962, the marshals enrolled James Meredith into the University of Mississippi. Meredith was assigned a room in the student dorm with twenty-four-hour protection. Even in his classes, the marshals were present or standing outside of the classroom.

One late morning, several days after Meredith's enrollment, several of my graduate student friends and I went to the grill in the student union to have coffee. We chose a table close to the entrance and I sat with my back to the door. Suddenly, the crowd of students sitting at the tables jumped up and darted to the exits. I wondered if the place was on fire. Turned around and in came James Meredith with two marshals. I nodded at him, and he smiled at me. We grads didn't jump up nor cared if Meredith came in or not. After he was seated, the students started re-entering the grill and took their original places. Soon the place got back to normal, and we guessed they realized that Meredith was no threat, and at least they made a showing. After a few weeks things were getting back to normal, and no one was talking about him.

One incident that disturbed me dealt with the press.

For days there was nothing to report. I had an office in the Lyceum building and the press were always hanging out on the steps waiting for something to happen. I came out one afternoon and saw the press across the street in the circle where the American flag waved every day.

I never trusted the press from watching them during this integration process, so I went over to see what was going on. There was a reporter and camera man. The reporter had the Rebel flag in his hand and asked two passing students to lower the American flag and hoist up the Rebel flag. I was proud of the boys, they declined and walked away. I could see the evening news: *Ole Miss students rebel, lowering the American flag and hoisting up the Rebel flag.* When there's no news, they try to create it. James Meredith graduated on August 18, 1963.

CHAPTER 27

Pharmacy Moves into Its New Building

In early spring of 1963, we got word that Hume Hall was now open and the College of Pharmacy, with its new dean, Dr. Charles Hartman, would be moving into its new building. Ed and I were assigned offices on the ground floor on the right side, close to the entrance, with separate doors to our offices. The back doors in our offices opened into a large common laboratory that Ed and I shared. It was ideal because Ed was great in the lab, and he would be a big help to me.

Next to my office were a series of offices, one of which became the new Dean's office. Further down from Dean Hartman's space was Dr. Lewis Nobles' Graduate Dean's office close to the door that went out into the parking lot. Across from his office was a classroom, and across from Dean Hartman's office was a small library and next to it moving up to the front were offices that ended at a large pharmacy laboratory.

On the second floor was the Medicinal Chemistry Department office with Dr. Joseph Sam as the chairman, several large laboratories, classrooms, and individual offices for graduate students.

On the third floor was the Microbiology Department.

My lab was well-stocked, and I began my research, trying for months to add a chemical group into the estrogen molecule without success. I went to the chemistry library and reviewed articles related to my research for assistance. For two months I ran several new chemical reactions but couldn't add the group I wanted into the estrogen molecule. Ed and I decided that the estrogenic compound couldn't be made.

In my next monthly meeting with Dr. Nobles, I reviewed my latest efforts in the lab. Then I suggested that the reaction we originally proposed probably wasn't going to work and I would like to develop something new. He agreed and suggested I review the literature and come up with a new project that I would like for his and my committee's approval.

There were times that Dr. Nobles would make trips to Washington, D.C. in search for grant money. During those times he asked me to teach a few lectures in his pharmacy math class held in the classroom across from his office. I found the experience rewarding and I needed the teaching experience. During that time, I met an intelligent young pharmacy student in the class, Dewey D. Garner, who became a future brother in Kappa Psi and eventually President of the Fraternity. In many of his talks he told the brothers that he was never good in pharmacy math because I taught him. That got him a lot of laughs.

My research now required that I spend weeks in the chemistry library to develop my new project finally titled: *Potential Anti-Infective Agents*. This project dealt with the synthesis of a series of chemical compounds that could be employed in the treatment of pathogenic invading organisms, which are known as chemotherapeutical agents. These chemical substances act upon invading pathogenic organisms with only a minimum detrimental effect upon the tissues and physiological processes of the host.

I developed 40 new chemical agents and their syntheses, but I had to get both Dr. Nobles' and my committee members' approval. Dr. Nobles reviewed my project first. He approved it and then instructed me to deliver copies to my committee. While I was waiting for their response, Dr. Nobles asked me to move into the new lab next to his office. A door in his office opened into the lab, which was a way for him to escape from someone he didn't want to see and was easy access out to the men's room. More importantly, it was convenient because we had conversations in the lab about my research without scheduling visits in his office.

I ordered supplies and started my research before receiving my committee's approval, which finally came one-by-one in the next few weeks.

The next year, in 1964, Ed received his Ph.D. and accepted a faculty position at the University of Rhode Island. I hated to see him and Sandy go but was happy that he had reached his goal, and they were starting a new life. In that same year I finished my course work but now as another requirement for the Ph.D. in medicinal chemistry, I had to complete my research project. This meant that I had to devote full time to the laboratory. For the next year and a half, I dropped Char off at the engineering department at eight in the morning and I went to the lab. At five o'clock, I'd pick her up and we'd go home and prepare dinner together and sit as a family with our four children. Then around seven every evening I went back to the lab and worked until midnight. This one evening when I made a right turn at the corner, a block from our house, heading to University Avenue, the iron spring under the left back fender of our Chevy fell out on the street. My car tilted to the left and I pulled over to the curb. I got out, walked over to it, and threw the spring into the trunk. I was glad that it was dark. I made it to the lab and the next morning I drove to a mechanic I knew, and he fixed it.

I took time on Saturday and Sunday to be with Charmaine and our children. Saturday night was the only time I didn't return to the lab. It was a precious time being with the family, but on Sunday around seven I had to get back in the lab. I felt bad but rationalized that I had to finish so we could move on, and I could build a better life for my family.

Dorothy with Magarian
Family Children

Bob in lab with his girls

Paula, Cindy, Leslie, & Bobby

Family with Grandma Magarian

CHAPTER 28
Writing My Ph.D. Dissertation

In early May of 1966, I finished my research project, and it was time to write my Ph.D. dissertation. At that time there were no photocopiers, no computers, no computer programs, no fax, only a mimeograph machine. After writing a second draft of my manuscript, it was ready to be typed. Wasn't so easy back then as it is today, using different computer programs to accomplish writing goals, such as a cut and paste key and a delete key.

Charmaine was my typist—after all we were working toward the Ph.D. together—she typed, and I drew the chemical structures. The typing was arduous. An original single sheet of bond paper with two onion skin sheets behind it as carbon copies. There was black carbon paper behind each sheet, except the last sheet. She rolled them all together into the typewriter. If a mistake were made, each page had to be individually erased and typed over. We worked for two weeks typing and drawing structures. She typed 103 pages, which included 9 tables of structural information—chemical names and analyses, and 36 pages of chemical reactions with structures. After I drew the structure, she had to add the chemical elements to each chemical structure attached and the reagents used in each reaction. The Experimental Section with each chemical name of all compounds that I synthesized in the lab with their elemental analyses and description of each chemical reaction was monumental. How she accomplished it all without turning grey-headed, I don't know. But she never complained. She was my angel.

This one Sunday in May, while still working on the dissertation all morning in our kitchen, which was our workstation, by noon I had had it. I asked Charmaine if she felt like taking a break and drive to Memphis, 90 miles away, to relax. She was ready and we gathered our children, and in our Chevy, we headed to Batesville to get on I55 north to Memphis. Before leaving the big city, I stopped for refreshments for everyone. The kids didn't know that I had a couple of beers in the package to drink while we worked to quiet my nerves. Back at our workstation, we continued long hours for several days and finally completed the dissertation.

We had to have four reading copies printed at the print shop for my Ph.D. committee members—Dr. Lewis Nobles, Dr. Joseph Sam, Dr. Norm Dorenbos, and Dr. W.R. Nes.

After giving them two weeks to read my dissertation, we scheduled my final committee meeting to present my work. I remember it well. Even though I had met with my committee many times before, this time was my last meeting to earn the Ph.D.

I felt confident but a little apprehensive. The day came in the latter part of May 1966. I met with the committee in one of the classrooms where I could use the chalkboard. My presentation went well, and then came the questions. I answered most but got stumped on one, and Dr. Nobles deliberately asked me a question he knew if I answered, it would lead me into answering the original question. He saved me. When they were done asking questions, Dr. Nobles asked me to leave the room. I waited out in the hall for about fifteen, twenty minutes. They were discussing my performance and progress and had to sign the original copy of my dissertation.

Dr. Nobles came out and said, "Congratulations, Dr. Magarian," and smiled. He led me back into the room to meet with my other committee members, who congratulated me. Dr. Nobles handed me the one copy with their signatures. The weight I felt earlier had lifted off my shoulders.

It was close to five o'clock and I hurried over to the Engineering Building where Charmaine was working for the Assistant Dean, Dr. Anderson. to pick her up behind the building. When she entered the passenger's side, she asked how my dissertation defense went. I told her, that they said I had to meet with them again. It didn't go too well. I saw the disappointment in her face and immediately said. "Only kidding. I passed. All went well."

Her face lit up with smiles and I leaned over and kissed her.

"I can't thank you enough Char for all your help."

The smile on her face warmed my heart. "I knew you'd do well. You work so hard."

It felt good to always have her support. Such a kind soul, my wife.

The next step was to have the print shop make copies of the signed dissertation. The original manuscript went to the Graduate College, a copy to the library, one for each of my committee members, one for Dr. Nobles as my major professor, and one for me.

In our medicinal chemistry seminar during my last two months in graduate school, Dr. Ed Smissman was the invited speaker. Smissman, a highly respected researcher, was chairman of the Medicinal Chemistry Department at the University of Kansas. I was so impressed with his research that after his presentation, I went up to talk with him about his research and my interests, I immediately asked Dr. Nobles if he'd talk with Dr. Smissman about me doing a postdoc with him. Nobles did, and Smissman was interested in me, and he directed me to apply for an NIH postdoctoral fellowship, which I did, and was awarded a two-year fellowship.

In early July of 1966, before my Ph.D. graduation, Charmaine and I loaded up our children in our old Chevy with the hole in the floor on the passenger's side, covered with a rubber mat so Char's feet wouldn't sink into the hole, and drove to Lawrence, some 565 miles from Oxford, to look over the campus and find a home to rent.

We arrived in Lawerence in early evening and found a motel close to campus. After checking in, we took a brief tour of the KU campus, looking for the Pharmacy building. Our plan was to find a house to rent close to the university. But house searching had to wait until morning, because we had four tired and hungry children -Paula 10, Cindy 8, Leslie 6, and Bobby 4. The next morning, we rose around eight and I went out for a Lawrence newsother paper before breakfast to scan houses for rent. During breakfast, Charmaine and I scanned the paper.

We found several and asked the desk clerk if he knew if any of the homes listed were close to the campus. He scanned the listings, circled the homes, and pointed to the one that was closest to the campus and near an elementary school. He even gave us directions. I called the number listed in the paper. The lady that answered was the owner. I gave her a summary of our background: how many children we had, their ages, and that I was going to be doing research at the University. She got quiet but didn't say anything. I wondered if it was because we had four children. I asked if we could meet in an hour. That gave us time to find the house and look over the neighborhood and the local school before we met. She agreed.

We liked the little brick home and the area. All the properties were in good shape and the lawns were well kept, and the school was only a couple of blocks away.

We pulled up behind the car in the driveway, got out and went to the door. The lady must have seen us through the large front window. She opened the door before I had a chance to knock. She greeted us with a smile. I thought her to be in her forties and Hispanic. She invited us in, and we followed her throughout the three-bedroom house. As we toured the place our children didn't run all over the place or make any noises. They stayed close to their mother.

When we ended up in the kitchen, I could tell from looking at Char that she liked the place. We were good at communicating with each other through facial expressions.

I told the lady we liked her house and would like to rent it. What was the rent? She hesitated at first, then told us. It was in our price range, and I told her it was okay. She pulled out a lease from a folder on the kitchen table and said she would only give us a one-year lease, which could be renewed if both parties were still in agreement. Which meant to me, if our children didn't tear up the place. After reading over the lease, Charmaine and I signed it and fortunately for us, she only required a deposit until we moved in. But if we changed our minds about moving in, we could lose our deposit.

We returned to Oxford and began planning our move.

The summer graduation was held in the Field House at 10 am this Saturday morning in July. Like all graduations, students marched in according to their school. I was with other Ph.D. students in the Graduate College, and we marched in last. As we moved down the center aisle, I waved and winked at Char and waved at our four children (Paula 10; Cindy 8; Leslie 6, and Bobby 4) as I passed by them. It felt good to see their smiling faces. I thought as I passed, *That's my lovely family.*

The ceremony was long because this was the first time the Law School hooded their graduates. When our time came, each Ph.D. student was hooded by their major professor (advisor). Dr. Nobles smiled at me as he hooded me and then shook my hand and congratulated me. I was now a Ph.D. Frankly, it felt good. When the ceremony concluded, I had my last visit with Dr. Nobles and thanked him for all he did for me and my family. Then I went to the back to meet my smiling family and give Charmaine a tightly held hug and a kiss as I whispered in her ear: "We made it! Love you and thanks for believing in me." Next, I hugged my little kiddos. I was so proud of my family. I believe we were the only ones with four children.

Charmaine and I had no other immediate family members present at our graduation but Ed and Sandy. My folks couldn't make it because mom was ill, and Charmaine's mother and father wasn't able. But to our surprise, Charmaine's Aunt Virginia and Uncle Floyd Rhodes from O'Fallon, Illinois, knocked on our door that evening as we were celebrating with several graduate students, devouring a huge cake and lots of punch.

The Floyds were pleased that I got the Ph.D. and wanted to surprise us and celebrate our accomplishment with us. Aunt Virginia was a writer and loved everything about higher education.

During the evening, I got a call from my dad, who congratulated me and called me *Dr. Magarian.* He was sorry they couldn't make it. I knew he really wanted to be with us. We did have an enjoyable conversation and the evening with the Floyds, Ed and Sandy, and several graduate students made for a joyous occasion.

Virginia & Floyd Rhodes

Bob, Dr. Lewis Nobles,
Dr. Ed Magarian

Dr. Robert A. Magarian

CHAPTER 29
Postdoc: University of Kansas

In early August 1966, I reported to the Department of Medicinal Chemistry in the College of Pharmacy and met with Dr. Smissman, Chairman of the department. He had one of the graduate students take me to a lab with six benches, all but one of which were occupied by graduate students and stacked with lots of glassware and research equipment. To the right of the room were four fume hoods against the entire wall.

I was taken to the last bench, which would be my workstation. Standing at the bench, I could see the parking lot behind the building. The graduate student introduced me to the students working at their benches and helped me get all the equipment I needed from the stockroom. Once I had everything I needed, I then met with Dr. Smissman to discuss the research project that I described in my fellowship application to NIH.

Over the months, our research went well, and I became friends with one of the students, Ron Borne, who was working on his Ph.D. research in a lab across the hall from ours. He was studying with one of the other professors in Med. Chem. I didn't know at the time that Ron Borne would become one of my best friends and an author friend in later years.

Paula, Cindy, and Leslie were enrolled in the elementary schools a few blocks from our home and had made new friends as we were enjoying our time in Lawerence, and at KU.

Besides doing research, the department had seminars and meetings in one of the classrooms where all graduate students gathered to sharpen their synthetic skills by solving synthetic reactions that Dr. Smissman would put on the board in front of the room. The body of students would divide into two groups and challenge each other as to the best chemical route to synthesize a particular compound. I found this quite stimulating.

I also sat in a course on synthetic organic chemistry. The professor was brilliant. He drew structures in chemical reactions on the blackboards without notes, starting at the left, filling all the boards without erasing once.

A few months before the end of my first year with Dr. Smissman, Charmaine and I realized that we couldn't stay a second year. We were struggling to stretch our budget, and we decided I needed to find a teaching job. I talked it over with Dr. Smissman and he was very understanding and recommended that I might inquire at the St. Louis College of Pharmacy. Their Dean, Charles Blissitt, had inquired if there was anyone interested in coming to his college.

Dr. Smissman was born and raised in East St. Louis, not far from my grandparents. He knew I was from the area and thought maybe I'd be interested in getting back in the home territory. I wasn't really interested in that nor taking a teaching job with the St. Louis College of Pharmacy because it wasn't a research school. After Charmaine and I discussed our options, we decided that maybe a few years teaching experience would help me when I applied for a teaching/research position in the future. In the back of my mind, I knew I wouldn't be staying at the St. Louis College of Pharmacy for long because research in breast cancer was my goal.

CHAPTER 30
Joining St. Louis College of Pharmacy Faculty

I had interviewed and accepted a position for fall of 1967, with the idea that I would eventually search for a pharmacy school known for its research after gaining teaching experience.

We rented a house one block south off Clayton Road in Clayton, Mo., west of Forest Park and close to Washington University, which I had attended in the '50s. Paula was 11 years old, Cindy 9, Leslie 7, and Bobby was 5. The girls were enrolled in the Clayton schools, which were excellent, and Bobby was a preschooler. Clayton road ran north and south in the City of Clayton and it bisected St. Louis Avenue one block north of our rental house.

Driving to work, I chose the shortest route, which was to travel east on St. Louis Avenue towards Washington University, enter Forest Park on a winding road that came out on Kingshighway Boulevard. A block away was the Pharmacy School.

After a couple of weeks, I convinced myself that the school was acceptable for a short term, but not for the long haul. The faculty were mostly graduates of the college and were close knit. I found this strange for a school to inbreed—hiring their own graduates after earning advanced degrees—to fill the faculty.

Our building was on the corner of Euclid Avenue across from Barnes and Jewish Hospitals. On the same side of the street as the college, a block away, was the Washington University Medical School.

The Pharmacy building was a single three-story building. My department and cubicle, no office, was on the third floor. I was assigned a carrel facing the physics teacher. I felt like I was in a high school environment. Not to my liking. The College taught all five years of courses, including the basic freshman courses.

After a year in our house, we had an opportunity in the summer of 1968 to move into a two-story brick building facing Clayton Road that was owned by a music school a few blocks away. We were given free rent to act as a mom-and-pop couple that supervised the girls attending the school and living in what we liked to call, "The Dorm."

My first year on the faculty, I taught Organic Chemistry with a lab. My class size was 110. This meant a lot of tests to grade and two lab sessions per week. At the end of the year, I failed five students in the course and was called into Dean Blissitt's office. He seemed a little nervous, which was a red flag, telling me that bad news was coming. I was right. He told me that Mr. Roby, the president of the college, looked over the grades and was disappointed that I failed students. The dean told me I needed to think about my grading system and that I would have to teach the five students in summer school but not the lab. That didn't set well with me. It was a sign of punishment, making the school even lower on my scale of satisfaction.

The second school year—1968-69—I taught Medicinal Chemistry and at the end of the spring semester, I failed six people. Several of the faculty and I were scheduled to attend the annual APHA (American Pharmaceutical Association) meeting, which this year was in Montreal, Canada. Before we left, I turned in my grades into the office.

At the APHA meeting each year, several faculty were invited to attend the Bucke Dinner, which was an enjoyable time interacting with Mr. and Mrs. Bucke. Mr. Bucke was a graduate of the College and owned a small Pharmaceutical Company in Indiana. They had the dinner at the best hotels, and it was an honor to be invited. Mrs. Bucke supervised the five-course dinner. She must leave a huge tip to the wait staff because they were hopping around like bunnies, seeking her approval on everything.

Eight of us were seated at a large round table with a white linen clothe, dressed like in the movies. The wait staff were hustling around to make sure Mrs. Bucke was pleased with the set-up and the service. Both she and her husband were very gracious and very likeable. We had two faculty members join us after we had the first course. They had just arrived from the airport and were served wine as we had our glasses refilled. While we were eating, a waiter came to Dean Blissitt and whispered something in his ear. He got up and left the table. While we were in an enjoyable conversation with the Bucke's, one of the faculty members who joined us late, vomited at the table. His companion quickly ushered him away from the table and the waiters hurriedly covered the vomit with white towels and cleaned up the mess. Mr. Bucke said he was sorry for the faculty member and hoped he was okay. Mrs. Bucke also felt bad for the faculty member. She tried to make him feel comfortable when they returned to the table. We all got back to our meal and when Dean Blissitt returned, he leaned over and said to me, "Bob, we need to meet when we get back to the college."

I knew what was coming.

On Monday morning after returning from the convention, I went to the Dean's office. As I entered, I could see from the expression on Dean Blissit and his body language that my time has come. I was going to the cross. After we were seated, he said, "Bob," then stopped for a few seconds, then said, "Mr. Roby was unhappy with your grades." He stopped again and sadly looked at me and said, "I'm sorry to tell you this, but he said you have a year to look for another job."

I knew this was coming but I didn't care. I was ready to leave. I had struggled to build a small research lab and was only able to get one research paper from working in the lab between classes.

When I got home and told Charmaine what had happened, she said, "I could tell you haven't been happy here. It's time for us to move on."

I thought, *Thank God for my sweet, supportive wife.*

137

CHAPTER 31

In Remembrance of My Mother: Pauline Struel Magarian

My mother and father lived across the river (Mississippi) in East Louis in a new duplex. My brother Leon lived next door with his wife Germaine and two daughters, Melanie and Julie. My dad was now retired.

During the winter of 1969, the beginning of my last year at the St. Louis College of Pharmacy, my father fell out of bed and hurt his thigh and was on the floor. My mother called us upset and almost in tears about the possibility of him breaking his hip. By the time we got there, Leon had gotten our dad back in bed and got him dressed. We were able to get him into the car and rushed to the hospital while Charmaine stayed with mom.

In the hospital he didn't appear to have broken his hip, but he complained about his thigh. While he was being attended to in the ER, we got a call from Charmaine. She said my mom thought she was having a heart attack. So, Leon and I hurried back and got her into the car. Charmaine and I were seated in the back. I sat behind mom holding her shoulders while she was asking about our dad, still worried about him more than herself. I was really worried about her and feared for her life. We got her to the ER, and they began treating her for a heart attack. I stayed with her until they took her to the intensive care unit. Then I went to my dad's room and sat by his bed. I looked at him and my heart ached. Here is my dad with his wife in intensive care and he in a bed and couldn't go see her. I told him Mom was here in the ER.

He looked at me and said, "What's wrong?"

"We think Mom may have had a heart attack," I said.

He looked up at the ceiling but didn't say anything.

I told him I'd keep checking on her and get back with him. They didn't allow us in the Intensive Care unit, which disappointed me greatly. My brother Leon was with me. By now my brother Ed and Sandy had arrived from Kentucky. We all went to our dad's room,

A couple hours later, I got word from the nurse that Mom wasn't doing well. I told my dad. He just stared into space. We both were in silence for some time. Ed and Sandy sat at the foot of Hydig's bed. Chamaine and Leon stood next to them.

I went to the intensive care unit and sat outside. Thirty minutes later I was told Mom had passed. I felt so bad that I wasn't allowed to be with her at that time to hold her hand. I wanted to kiss her and thank her for all she did for us. I went with a heavy heart to tell our dad. I sat with him, and he only looked up at the ceiling without saying a word. I could only imagine, here's my father, who couldn't be with his wife of 46 years when she passed. What was he thinking? What would I be thinking if I were in his situation? So many thoughts would have gone through my mind, worst of all, not being with her to tell her I loved her.

We called Kassly's Funeral home and when the attendants came, we asked them to roll the gurney with her body into my dad's room so he could say goodbye. After aligning her gurney next to his bed and unzipping the black leather bag to expose her head, they left the room. I held my dad up by his shoulders close to her so he could bend over to see Mom. He kissed his hand and place it on her face, and said, "I'll be joining you soon."

Tears flowed down our faces. I laid him back down and went around his bed to the gurney and bent over and kissed my mother on her forehead and laid my face on hers. *Thanks for all you did for us, Mom! I love you!*

I motioned for the funeral attendants to take my mother.

My dad still wouldn't be released from the hospital for several days.

We went back to Leon's duplex. I called my uncle Magarian's family, and told Aznive, my cousin, that mom had died. She immediately came to see us, visibly shaken. She and my mother were the greatest of friends and I could see the sadness in Aznive's eyes. She couldn't believe she lost her best friend. Of course she wanted to know what had happened. We told her the entire story.

We planned mom's funeral with our dad, but unfortunately, he couldn't attend. Aznive took his place and rode with us in the limousine to St. Henry's Catholic Church. There was a huge crowd. After the service, the church ladies' group prepared a meal for family and friends in the lower level of the church.

Later that evening, I went to the hospital to tell Hydig about the beautiful funeral and who all were there. I felt sad for him. He said very little.

When he was discharged from the hospital, we didn't want him to live alone in his side of the duplex. Both Leon and Germaine worked so my dad came to live with us. We gave him our room in our two-bedroom apartment on Clayton Road. We put another bed in the second room, so we could sleep in the same room with Leslie and Bobby, while Paula and Cindy slept in the living room on the couch that opened into a nice bed.

CHAPTER 32
Seeking a New Teaching/Research Position

During the remaining months of the 1969 school year at the College, I informed Dr. Smissman and Dr. Nobles that I was looking for a teaching/ research position. Soon after, I got an offer to interview with Dean Glasser at the University of Cincinnati College of Pharmacy, which was a good research school. I knew Dr. Glasser through my brother Ed, who was on the faculty with Glasser in Kentucky before he became dean at the University of Cincinnati. I accepted the offer to go to Cincinnati for an interview.

A few days before I was ready to leave for Cincinnati, Dean Blissitt called me into his office. When I entered, he pointed for me to take a seat while he was at his desk on the phone. When he hung up, he asked me how I was doing. "Okay," I said, wondering what was going on. He seemed to be going out of his way to be nice. He came around from his desk and took a seat facing me. He smiled and asked if I had accepted a position anywhere. I told him I hadn't, but I was going to Cincinnati for an interview. He squirmed in his chair a little. Dean Blissitt never seemed very confident in his position. I believed it was because the president, Mr. Roby, was always looking over his shoulder.

To my surprise, he told me he was leaving the college. It took a few minutes for it to sink in. *What happened to him*, I thought. *Was he fired?* Anything was possible with Mr. Roby at the helm. Then he told me he had accepted the Dean's position at the University of

141

Oklahoma College of Pharmacy in Norman.

"Congratulations," I said

He only smiled.

Then he asked if Charmaine and I would be willing to meet with him and his wife, Gail this coming Thursday in Norman, Oklahoma to spend the weekend to visit the college of Pharmacy and the campus. He would pay our expenses.

I thought about it for a minute without answering.

"I'm creating a new position in Medicinal Chemistry, and I'd like for you to fill that position."

I told him I'd have to talk it over with Charmaine and thought she might be willing to take a trip to Oklahoma. I emphasized that I couldn't consider his offer until I visited Cincinnati.

"That'll be fine," he said. "I'd like for you to look over what Oklahoma has to offer before you make up your mind."

When I arrived at home that evening, I told Charmaine about Blissitt's invitation to visit Oklahoma. She was in favor of going to visit Norman to look over the town, the homes, and their schools. I researched the history of the University and the College of Pharmacy and its faculty. I didn't recognize any of the names on the faculty nor the one faculty member in my field of Medicinal Chemistry.

Pharmacy was the first professional program at the University of Oklahoma in 1893 as a two-year regimen, graduated its first students in 1896. Formerly established as a School of Pharmacy in 1899, with Edwin C. DeBarr as dean. It continued as a two-year program. In 1907 the School of Pharmacy first offered a four-year Bachelor of Science degree.

We arrived in late afternoon on Thursday, checked into a motel and then drove around the town. Charmine and I found the town to be pleasant and not too busy like we were used to in St. Louis. That evening we met the Blissitt's for dinner and discussion. The dean was really giving me a sales pitch to come to Oklahoma.

I thought, *I gotta see the facilities, the faculty, and who is doing research.*

Friday morning Char went with Mrs. Blissitt and a realtor to look over homes close to schools suited for our four children. Blissitt and

I went to the college where we met in Dean Harris's office. He was a tall, lanky gray-haired man who didn't smile much. I got the feeling he wasn't too happy to see me. He told me there was no position in the college for me. But after we left his office Blissitt told me not to worry about what Harris said. He had the approval of the provost, Dr. Pete Kyle McCarter, who was originally from Mississippi. When we met with him, I told him about Ole Miss being my alma mater, and that brought smiles. He was a big Ole Miss fan.

He was very cordial and said he hoped I would join the faculty at OU. We then met with President Herbert Holloman. Rarely do potential faculty members ever meet with the president of the university. He was very informal and he, too, was very cordial. And like Dr. Pete, what many called him, I liked the president immediately. He was very casual and treated me like I was a Nobel Laureate. When we finished the visit, he said he hoped I would join their faculty.

After lunch, we went to the Pharmacy college and visited with each faculty member in their offices. Most of the faculty were of retirement age, which meant that Dean Blissitt would be hiring new faculty. He made sure to emphasize that the new hires would be research faculty, The old-timers on the faculty didn't seem too happy to see me, either and weren't too cordial. I knew they were threatened by new faculty since the old timers were a close-knit group. Only the faculty in pharmacology were doing research and were glad to hear I might be coming. When we discussed the pharmacology department among the old faculty, I sensed they felt threatened by them.

On the floor where I would do research, there was very little research equipment, but there were two big laboratories, one for teaching Drug Assay that was being phased out from the curriculum. The other lab was used by one faculty member in chemistry who taught four or five medical students, which only required the use of the first lab bench of the six. Blissitt assured me that I could use one of the two labs for my research if I came, and that it would take time to hire new faculty. Charmaine and I left with a good feeling. I thought I could get things done if the dean kept his promises. I didn't want another situation like I had in St. Louis.

A week later, Charmaine and I traveled to Ohio to visit the

University of Cincinnati College of Pharmacy located in the Health Sciences Center (HSC) downtown. When we got close Cleveland, the road circled down a hill and into the city, Charmaine got quiet. I knew what she was thinking.

This is no Norman, Oklahoma.

When we drove into the area around the college, we both became quiet. The HSC was surrounded on three sides by poor rundown areas. We pulled into the Faculty House where we would be staying as instructed over the phone by Art Glasser. It had a high fence and was locked at night. We met with the Glassers for an enjoyable dinner to get oriented on the next two days. Charmaine would be spending time with Mrs. Glasser and especially looking at homes. The next morning, we had breakfast and Charmaine went with Art's wife, and he and I went to the college where we met in his office. Art provided me with brochures about the HSC and the college. I learned that the college was a commuter school. There were classes during the night as well. When the day people left, the night students and faculty came. The faculty as well as students had to hunt and peck for parking spaces. He gave me a sheet that included the itinerary for the day. We left his office and met in one of the classrooms, where the dean introduced me to the faculty and then I made a forty-minute presentation about my research. I noticed in the audience a faculty member I knew from my postdoc days at Kansas. Art scheduled several of us for lunch, and while we were all learning about each one's research, my Kansas colleague leaned over to me and said he hoped I would come and work on a project with him.

After lunch, Art took me around to look over the campus and then we went into the provost's office. Art introduced me and we sat in two leather chairs facing him. I noticed he had my CV on his desk. He was probably in his early sixties, slender, and had a young-looking face, He wore a very expensive grey suit. He complimented me as he gazed over my CV. He looked up at Art and said, "Let's get Dr. Magarian to join us." Then he looked at me, and said he hoped I would come on board. I only nodded.

We left and Art dropped me off at the faculty house, where I could rest until dinner. When Char returned, I could tell from her demeanor that she wasn't happy. "How was your day?" I asked

"Not good." She continued telling me that the area in the city was not very nice and to live in a good area we'd have to go 30 miles out of town. She didn't like what she saw and wondered if I was really thinking about taking the job here. We paused to give me time to consider her feelings. I told her that while Norman was a beautiful town and the schools were great for our kids, I wasn't impressed with the OU Pharmacy facilities. While I didn't like the area in Cincinnati, their research facilities and research faculty were what I was looking for.

I could see that she looked despondent. She reminded me that Dean Blissitt did offer me a promotion to associate professor and supplies for research, and he did say he was going to hire other faculty.

I knew she was trying to paint a picture of a better situation. I told her if nothing else materializes, we will go to Oklahoma. She smiled and said she loved Norman.

The next morning, I had an exit visit with Dean Glasser. He offered me an associate professorship position, a couple thousand dollars increase in salary, and a lab with a lot of supplies. It was an enticing offer. I asked if I could have a week to think it over. He agreed.

When we got back to St. Louis, Dean Blissitt called me in and asked if I had accepted the position at Cincinnati? I told him I hadn't decided. I was thinking it over. He must have talked with Art because he tried to show me how he was up on things. He made the same offer as Art Glasser if I came with him to Oklahoma. I told him I would let him know.

In the meantime, I got a call from my former major professor, Dr. Lewis Nobles, Dean of the Graduate College at Ole Miss, who now was president of Mississippi College in Clinton, MS, which is a private Baptist university, and the oldest college in Mississippi. He invited me and Char down to see if I'd like a position in the chemistry department.

We took a long weekend and went to Clinton and stayed with the Nobles in the president's house. After spending the day at the college with Dr. Nobles, we visited in his office. I told him, while the chemistry department was interesting, I was looking for more medicinal chemistry faculty doing research. He agreed and I believe wanted to help if I didn't find a place. He was always kind and looking out for his students.

We went back to St. Louis with the intent of accepting Blissitt's offer even though I felt it wasn't the kind of environment I was looking for. It was going to take years to build the kind of department I wanted. I couldn't wait forever but had no other offers. I thought hard about what to do. I called everyone I knew. The only other possibility was to go into a pharmaceutical company. I didn't like industry. A couple of days passed, and I still was skeptical about going to Oklahoma, but we accepted the offer from Blissitt. He was so excited, I thought he was going to kiss me on the cheek.

CHAPTER 33

Bound for The University of Oklahoma

In late May 1970, after taking Hydig to Leon's home, Char and I, with Paula, Cindy, Leslie and Bobby, drove to Norman, over five hundred miles away. We checked into the same motel we stayed in during our first visit. The next morning, we allowed the kids to watch TV and play games while we planned to go around with the realtor looking at homes in neighborhoods with good schools. We got an early start and went through three homes. In between our day of house hunting, we checked on our children. At the end of the day, we went out and had a family dinner.

We liked a house on Mercedes Dr. and the next day the realtor made arrangement for us to tour the house. It had 2500 square feet, two bedrooms and a full bath upstairs; and two bedrooms and a full bath and a half downstairs. It was built two years earlier in 1968. The owners were the Mintons. The husband/father was an AirForce General stationed at Tinker Airforce Base, who was being transferred to California. Mrs. Minton, a middle-aged brunette with a narrow face, smiling brown eyes, and slender body was very pleasant and easy to work with. When we toured her house, I knew now how she stayed slender—raising five boys, who were upstairs in their rooms when she took us to look over the top floor.

Char first thought the house was a little more than we could afford, I convinced her that if this was the one she wanted, we should get it, even if it meant we wouldn't have enough furniture at first to fill it. All that Charmaine did for me, I wanted her to have the house she loved. I finally convinced her. We worked out a plan with the owners to hold a second mortgage on the property for six months. They agreed.

After spending another day in Norman with an attorney and Mrs. Minton finalizing all the paperwork, the Mercedes house became our first home. Char and I were elated. We stood in the front yard holding hands. Was this really ours? We looked at each other and realized that together we can do anything.

Returning to St. Louis, we began packing our things and decided that we'd be ready for the movers to pick up our possessions in the second week of June. Before leaving St. Louis, we traded our '54 Chevy in for a second-hand, newer model. We took my dad to stay with brother Leon and family until brother Ed and his wife Sandy, who had planned on coming to Norman for a visit, could bring him to Norman.

We arrived in Norman before the movers and opened our new home for them before they arrived. It took a couple of weeks to settle into our new home. The Blissitts lived one street over from us on Merkle, and their son, Bobby, maintained our lawn while we were in St. Louis.

Toward the end of June, Ed and Sandy arrived with Hydig. We eagerly waited for his reaction to his new home. He was slow-moving, but still able to make his way into the house on his own. He looked around as he walked through the foyer and came into the den area. He went into the living room and then into the kitchen and smiled, and said, "This is a beautiful home." We felt elated because we were indebted to him for helping us with our down payment.

"This is your home now," we told him.

We placed all his things in the master bedroom on the first floor, and we occupied the second bedroom down the hall while Paula, Cindy, Leslie, and Bobby took up residence in the large bedroom and the smaller one on the second floor. It felt good to see our family settle into our new environment.

During the weeks that we adjusted to our home, my dad and I sat on the couch in the evening and talked. He had asked me several times during our talks about my mother's funeral. She died in 1969, and he couldn't attend. He had fallen and was being treated in the hospital. It broke my heart to look into his eyes to see how he missed my mother, who he was married to for nearly fifty years. Emotions began to rise in me as I did the best I could to tell him that mom had a wonderful funeral, but he wanted to know who all were there and how the service was. I told him everything in detail and that his niece, Aznive, took his place and rode with us in the limousine to the church and to mom's grave site. I added that we had a nice meal for our relatives and friends at the church. It took a couple more times of describing what I could before he was satisfied.

CHAPTER 34

First Day at The OU College of Pharmacy

The first Monday in July, I left our new home and drove to the OU campus, about ten minutes away, and parked behind the Pharmacy building. Before leaving my car and entering the building, I got this uncanny feeling about my office. I never thought about it until now and wondered where they were going to put me since I never saw any vacant offices when I interviewed earlier. I left my car, walked around the building, up four wide concrete steps in front, entered through two large doors and took the stairs up to the second floor that led to the Dean's office. The door was open, and I could see a young man talking to a middle-aged woman seated at a desk close to the entrance. I entered and they both turned and looked at me. I introduced myself and learned that the young man, Dr. Walter Stanaszek, was a recently hired faculty member, too. The lady seated at her desk was the assistant dean, Dr. Blanche Sommers. She looked at us with surprise on her face, and said, "Oh, my, we've got to get you men desks and supplies."

She reached for her phone and placed a call.

Dean Blissitt had come out of his office to greet us while Dr. Sommers was on the phone. He invited us into his office.

This wasn't a good sign, I thought. *No desks meant no offices. I think I may have made a mistake coming here.*

Dean Blissit welcomed us, introduced Walter to me, and said he was hired for the clinical area. Clinical Pharmacy was in its infancy, and he explained that Walter would be taking students to OKC, 20 miles north to the Health Sciences Center (HSC). I learned during our conversation that Walter was from Chicago, 300 miles north of where I was born and raised. Blissitt took us out to meet up with Dr. Sommers, who told us that our desks were delivered, and they were put in the instrument room.

Another bad sign.

We followed her down to the first floor, walked to our left and down the hall to the instrument room. She opened the door, and we entered. The room was narrow but deep and the desks were shoved up against one another along the wall on the left. Counters on both walls extended to the back of the room. An infrared (IR) instrument was on the counter at the left wall, a few feet down from our desks. There was an assortment of supplies on the right wall counter.

A few office supplies were on our desks and all drawers were empty. There were no phones in the room. When I told Dean Blissitt we needed a phone, he smiled and said, "I'll get you two cans with a string attached."

We didn't think that was funny.

Walter and I looked at each other, We both knew what the other was thinking.

What the hell was this? No office. No phone.

After his joked bombed, Blissitt said he'd have a phone installed.

During that first day several faculty members came into our so-called office to welcome us—Dr. Ralph Clark, the former dean before Harris, had an office across from the instrument room next to a big lab, which I had my eye on. Dr. Richard Grunder, a medicinal chemist, who was very capable, but wasn't interested in research even though he had earned his Ph.D. from Purdue University and done a postdoctoral fellowship at Ohio State University. When I visited his office at the lower level of the building, I saw he had a fume hood in which there were round-bottom flasks positioned on cork rings. It appeared he started a reaction a decade ago and left the unclean glassware as it was.

He's not a researcher, I thought.

CHAPTER 35
Making Progress in The College

During the next two weeks I looked over my research notebooks and studied the project I wanted to start but needed lab space.

I remembered that the only other chemist on the faculty was Dr. Bruce, who had an office across from the instrument room next to Dr. Clark's. He used only the front bench in the large lab next to Clark's office, for teaching several medical students, but the other five benches and three fume hoods were not being used. I learned from Clark that Bruce hadn't taught the course in a year because the med students no longer were interested in his course.

I visited with Dean Blissitt to tell him I needed to use part of Bruce's lab for my research, and would he please talk to him. Blissitt wanted me to be diplomatic in dealing with Bruce so as not to offend him. I thought he should be a big boy by now—months away from retirement and I mentioned the lab wasn't in use.

I didn't talk to Bruce. Instead, I chose to use the last lab bench closest to the back wall with its fume hood against the wall. I called physical plant to come and check all three fume hoods to make sure they were working up to standard. Dr. B was watching my every move. He asked what I was doing. I told him I was using the back bench for my research and needed the hoods checked out. I could tell he didn't like it, but I didn't care. I checked on his background. He never did research nor publish anything outstanding. He acted like he owned the lab. I politely told him I needed to get started on my breast cancer research.

Surprisingly, he seemed interested and was a gentleman and left me alone after that. Soon I was managing the entire lab. I bought glassware, equipment and supplies, some of which I got from the stock room, and I expanded using the other benches. Now I had a nice lab to work in. Dr. B would come by often to see what I was doing and became impressed with the lab and told me so. On the surface, it appeared that he started to like me.

It took a couple of weeks, but Dr. Clark stopped by the instrument room and told Walter and I to draw straws, and the winner could share his office with him. He was retiring at the end of the school year. Walter told me to take it because I was using the lab, and the office was convenient. So, we pushed my desk into Clark's office against his desk where we would be facing each other. At the end of the school year Dr. Clark retired and I had the office to myself. Now I felt like I was making headway. It took six months to get my lab up and running. In 1972 I took on my first masters student, Eric Benjamin, and my second masters student, John Stobaugh two years later, both were outstanding students who went on to earn their Ph.Ds. at the University of Kansas. The Ph.D. graduate program in our college hadn't been approved and rightly so. There wasn't enough faculty in medicinal chemistry.

My teaching of medicinal chemistry was shared with Dr. Grunder, who taught one course, and I taught the other and then we'd switch. My first class consisted of many mature students, some of whom were veterans. I enjoyed the class because they were diligent. In my second year, the students weren't as interested in chemistry and there was some complaining that I was too hard. Like my classes in St. Louis, there were a few failures but not much was said about it. In my third year, an interesting thing happened. On Good Friday, Char and I attended noon service at St. John's Episcopal Church. When she and I returned to the college, there was a student standing on the steps holding up a sign that had a message to the president, Dr. Sharp. It read: *Dr. Magarian flunks half of his class and should be fired.*

We just walked past him as he tried to hold the sign up at us as we passed him to enter the building. I didn't know him. He wasn't in any of my classes. Char and I headed to my office, where two students were waiting outside my door. As we entered the office, the students told me that Doug got up in front of Dr. F's class and took class time to ask the students to sign a petition to get Dr. Magarian fired. They, and a few other students were unhappy with Doug and for Dr. F allowing him to do it during class time. No one signed the petition. I thanked the students for their support and immediately went to the provost's office. He told me to see Dr. Martin Jischke, professor in the School of Aerospace, Mechanical and Nuclear Engineering, and President of the local chapter of the AAUP (American Association of University Professors). Jischke was pleasant and easy to talk with. We had a great discussion. He said we could have F's head, but did I want to go after him since he was old and ready for retirement. He could have a heart attack. I told him that I didn't want that, and I'd talk to Dean Blissitt to see if he would carry out my demands, and I'll hold off for a bit. He thought that was the best way to go.

I called Dr. F that evening, asking him why he did what he did. He tried to act as if it were no big deal and was condescending. I told him he hadn't heard the last of it.

I had my meeting with the dean, who was shocked, and I told him what Martin Jischke had said and that I didn't want to go that route. Blissitt was pleased I didn't. I told him if Dr. F did three things I wouldn't take the case to AAUP.

First, I wanted him to stand in front of his class and apologize to me using my name, for allowing Doug to use his class time to discuss a petition. Secondly, I wanted him to face me in my office and apologize. Thirdly, I wanted Dr. F to stand up at the next faculty meeting and apologize to me in front of the faculty. Interestingly, at the next faculty meeting, Dr. F. got up and said he had something to say. He stood in front of me an apologized to me for allowing a student to take class time to ask the class to sign a petition against me. He had large sweat stains under his arms showing through his white shirt. This told me it was wise not to proceed with any action through the AAUP.

Interestingly, Dr. Grunder gave Doug the failing grade. We determined that Doug was going to be in my class and was afraid he wouldn't pass again and probably be expelled. His father was on the board of pharmacy, and I presumed Doug felt he had power behind him. Politics was heavy in the College of Pharmacy and maybe the older faculty were afraid in some way. I wasn't.

This is not the end of the story.

I got a call that Dean Blissitt wanted to meet with me. I went to his office and sat facing him. He shook his head and told that he and I were to pick a committee of four faculty members to review my teaching and grading system as per the instructions of the new provost, Dr. Hunsberger. When he visited our college after being hired, it was clear Dr. I. Moyer Hunsberger, being an organic chemist, wasn't impressed with out college nor its faculty. As far as I was concerned, the feeling was mutual.

Politics at work in the college, I thought.

So, the dean and I picked four faculty members, who met in my office. Feeling embarrassed, they didn't know where to begin. I told them I would provide them my grades for the last two classes and my grading system to review and they could write their report. They were pleased because they had a scheduled meeting with Hunsberger in a few days. They reviewed all that I gave them and wrote a report.

After their meeting with Provost Hunsberger, the faculty committee came to my office. I could tell from their demeanor the meeting didn't go well. Hunsberger told them their report wasn't acceptable and to go back and redo it. They were shocked, thinking they had done a respectable job. I read their report, which covered my grading system, my grades given in two classes, and the number of students that failed.

I realized if this wasn't what Hunsberger wanted, then it could only mean one thing. He wanted me out of the way so Doug could have free sailing. I told the committee I knew what the provost wanted. He wanted them to write in their new report: *Dr. Magarian will not teach the course for two years.* They couldn't believe that's what the provost wanted.

I told them to write it and see. When they met with the provost again, he said, "Now that's a good report."

Weeks later, Dean Blissitt saw me in the hall outside my lab and asked if we could step into my office, he'd like to talk to me. I went behind my desk, pulled out my high-back leather chair, sat, and faced him while he chose the only other chair in the room. He wondered if we could do something for the students to get past the Doug case. He went on to say that he knew I was big in the Kappa Psi Pharmaceutical Fraternity at the St. Louis College of Pharmacy and wondered if I'd be willing to reactivate the local chapter, Gamma Omicron, as the faculty advisor. Blissitt was a brother in Kappa Psi so I could see where he was coming from. It was a great idea, and I was all in. He was thrilled that I accepted the role.

I contacted The Central Office and followed the process for reactivating Gamma Omicron. After filling out the paperwork, I was allowed to recruit students. I enticed twenty male students to join the largest pharmaceutical fraternity in the U.S. Before Grand Regent Bill Fitzpatrick (the President) arrived at the initiation weekend to speak to us, and to present us with the Chapter Charter, I had the group select a slate of officers. Our new chapter president thanked Bill Fitzpatrick, who was great at mixing with the new Brothers. The event was very rewarding and ended with a barbecue in Dean Blissitt's backyard.

A couple of years later I got a call from a medicinal chemist friend who was on the faculty in a Pharmacy School in Boston. He was chosen to be on a faculty-wide committee at a Boston University to find a provost. Hunsberger was applying.

Now's my chance.

I told my friend that Hunsberger didn't like Pharmacy and what he thought about our college and what he did to me. I just stated the facts. Not too surprising, Hunsberger wasn't chosen for the position.

One's actions will eventually have consequences, which they will have to deal with eventually.

CHAPTER 36

In Remembrance of My Father: Dr. Leon Magarian

My father was 91 and needed to be cared for more fully. Even though he was able to walk some and go to the bathroom, we got him a wheelchair to take him to different appointments. Charmaine took care of him during the day, made his meals and administered his meds. I was able to bathe and help him get dressed before I left for work. He made me proud of Char when he told everyone how well she took care of him, like his own daughter. We eventually got an in-home caretaker to help Char a couple of days a week.

During the middle of the night in the Spring of 1973, Hydig called out for me, sounding in great pain. I hopped out of bed, rushed into his room, and found him on the floor. He had gotten out of bed to go to the bathroom, slipped and fallen. He told me he thought he had broken his femur. I immediately got him up and into his wheelchair without hurting him and rushed him to the ER were they immediately rolled him into X-ray.

I remember well the interesting interaction between my father and our primary care physician, Dr B, who had taken care of my dad when he first came to Norman and both doctors had bonded. While we were in one of the stalls waiting for a diagnosis, Dr. B, came in and explained that there was a fracture in the femur (thighbone), the longest, and strongest bone in the body. Haydig, lying on the bed, looked up at Dr.

B and asked him if the greater trochanter was involved. The greater trochanter with its head (ball) and neck connect to the pelvis. Dr. B responded holding his right hand up in a fist to resemble a ball shape turned inward representing the great trochanter and said, "If you mean the ball head and neck of the femur attached to the pelvis, no it wasn't involved."

I found this amusing that my dad had studied gross anatomy seventy years earlier, but still knew his gross anatomy.

Hydig had to have surgery and screws were used to hold the bones in their correct position. He was in a physical therapy facility for two weeks and then I brought him home. He was doing well for a while, but then complained about the screws were protruding up under his skin. I examined the area of the leg and could see screw heads bulging under the skin.

I got in touch with the surgeon, who came to the house. Interestingly, he stood at the foot of my dad's bed while I exposed my dad's leg to point at the area. He didn't approach my dad to look at the messed-up job he had done. All he said was that he would need to go back in and fix it.

No, you aren't, I thought. *You shouldn't be allowed to operate on patients.*

We got a different surgeon through our family doctor. Later I learned that the surgeon who screwed up my dad's leg was no longer allowed to do surgery at the hospital.

In the Fall of 1973, my dad and I were sitting on the couch together and I noticed he was feeling his back and upper abdominal area and he said, "I think I have cancer." Being a physician, I knew how great a diagnostician he was, for I had worked with him for four years while in high school. We went to the doctor, and he was correct. He had pancreatic cancer. They did surgery, but just closed him up. Nothing could be done. He lived a miserable two months, and he had to be transported back to the hospital. Two days later, I got a call that he had died. I told the nurse not to have his body moved until we got there. We had to see him. When we arrived, the funeral director assistants had Hydig in a body bag, which I asked him to unzip. I rubbed my hand over his bald head and bent over to give him my goodbye kiss. Charmaine did the same.

"Thank you for all you did for us, Hydig!"

We had his body shipped back to East St. Louis to be buried next to my mother. My brothers and I arranged a nice funeral for him with a gathering and meal in Leon's home after the funeral.

After my dad died, Charmaine went to work at the OCCE (Oklahoma Center for Continuing Education) on the Norman campus in different departments for seven years. In the '70s we found my salary didn't go far since the faculty hadn't had a raise in two straight years. Char's contribution helped us survive.

In 1975 Dean Blissitt resigned over some conflict and the College of Pharmacy was placed under the authority of the Health Sciences Center (HSC) Provost, since the college would be moving to the HSC in Oklahoma City in a year.

During that year Charmaine and I and family got a great surprise. Dr. Saul Levinson, one of our faculty members, and his wife Janet, invited us to their home for a weekend to celebrate one of their friend's 25th Wedding Anniversary. We were told some of our faculty, a former Dean and wife, along with many other of their friends would be there. So, we dressed in our Sunday best, and it was a good thing we did, because the friends they were honoring was us—our 25th wedding Anniversary. What a surprise!

When we arrived, we were greeted by Charmaine's aunt Virginia and Uncle Floyd from Illinois. John Zuzack, a colleague of mine when I was on the faculty at the St. Louis College of Pharmacy, and his wife Elaine, the former Dean Dr. Clark and wife, and several of our College of Pharmacy faculty members. I had wondered how Dr. Levinson and Janet got the addresses of those from out of town. Later, I learned that they got them from Charmaine who was in on the planning.

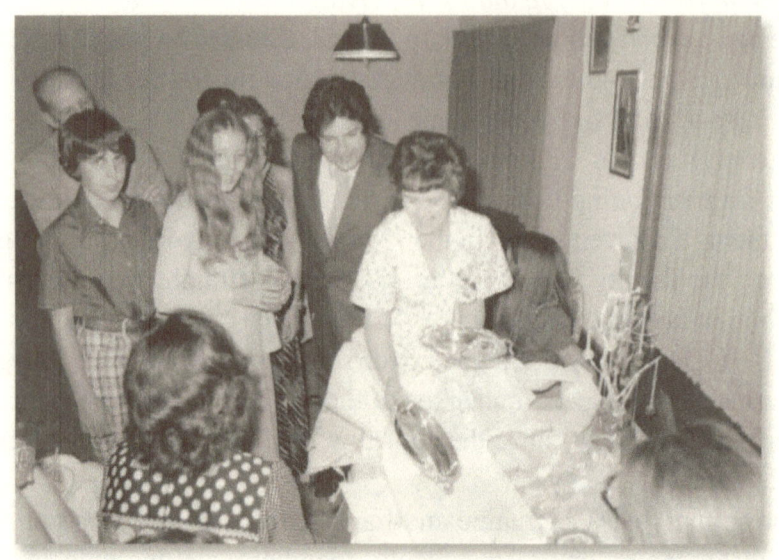

Bob & Charmaine's 25th Anniversary

*Dr. Saul & Janet Levinson, hosts of Bob & Char's
25th Wedding Anniversary*

Floyd & Virginia Rhodes with Bob & Char

*The Magarian children celebrating their father
and mother's 25th Wedding Anniversary*

CHAPTER 37
College of Pharmacy Moves to Oklahoma City

The provost in the Health Sciences Center (HSC) in Oklahoma City appointed Dr. John Sokatch, a professor in Microbiology and Biochemistry, as our interim dean in 1975. He occupied the dean's office for one year, and in July 1976, the college moved to the HSC in homes on 13th street, because our building hadn't been built. Dr. Rodney D. Ice (1976-1983) was selected as our new dean.

Each department occupied separate houses on both sides of 13th street, one block from the hospital, which were previously occupied by dental departments until they got their new building. The homes were originally built by physicians who worked at the hospital.

With the new dean, the politics diminished, and new faculty were hired. The college was taking on a new appearance and perspective. Dean Ice hired Richard Shough as his associate dean.

While we weren't in our new pharmacy building, we did remarkably well, communicating and carrying out our mission. We taught our classes in the auditorium in the School of Public Health, a block away. To keep the students together, I continued my support of the Gamma Omicron Chapter of Kappa Psi as their faculty advisor. We had meetings, initiated new members, and had banquets honoring students and faculty. Even without a building we were very cohesive.

In fall of 1976, I got a call that my brother Leon had passed from a heart attack at the age of 47. It took me several months to recover from my silent grief. He and I were like twins. We were only a year apart in age and for five days in the year we were the same age. We did so much growing up together. Here are a couple of tales about him.

I'd like to tell a story about what Mom used to say to me and Leon. "You boys are going to be the death of me yet."

This one summer afternoon, on a Sunday after church, Leon and I dressed in new white outfits and new shoes—mom liked us dressed as twins—we went across the street from our home to Jone's Park. It was a beautiful park with a lagoon that circled a pavilion in which an orchestra played music all afternoon. There were row boats and canoes that lovers and families would guide along listening to the music. It was a peaceful time. Leon was probably 12 and I was 11. We walked along the lagoon and headed to the bridge that crossed over to the pavilion, a large refreshment stand, and a baseball field. There were no row boats to rent so we got a canoe. We hopped in and paddled to the bridge that was 20 yards away. When we got under the bridge the canoe overturned. Don't know what caused it but after pushing the overturned canoe off our heads we were standing in water up to our chest. I could feel the goldfish swimming around my legs and being quite mad. Leon said, "I've lost one shoe." We went down under the water to search for it but couldn't find it in all the mud. I said, "Mom is going to kill us."

We struggled pushing the canoe through the water back to the pavilion. We hopped out and headed home. I kept saying, "Mom is going to kill us." As we crossed over the bridge and walked along the lagoon we unfortunately met up with our neighbors. The lady said, "Oh my. Your mother isn't going to be happy with you boys." I guess not, since we had mud all over our new white outfits and Leon was walking with only one shoe on. We didn't need to hear her comments. We had enough fear in us.

As we crossed the street and went to our home, I kept saying, "Mom is going to kill us." When we entered the house, I hid behind Leon. Mom gasped. "What happened to you boys?" We told her. Her facial expression told us what was coming next.

"You boys are going to be the death of me yet."

We pleaded our case: it wasn't done on purpose. "Where is your other shoe?" she asked Leon. He told her. "Go back and get that shoe!" she said, almost screaming. "But, mom, it's in the water." "I don't care! Those are new shoes. Go back now and find that shoe!"

Well, you guessed it. We weren't going to jump into the water and look for a shoe. The park cops wouldn't be too happy with us. We went back to the park and sat by the lagoon watching the row boats and canoes glide by. I noticed that Leon was still wearing only one shoe. We were so shaken that he didn't think about putting on other shoes. After an hour, we went back home. Mom had calmed down and she grabbed us and hugged us and said, "Thank God you boys didn't drown. We can always buy more shoes."

Another story.

When Leon and I were in our teens, we began experimenting with cigarettes. Our dad, the physician, smoked Camel cigarettes. Now, before you start passing judgment on our dear dad, you must realize everything was different in the forties. Doctors smoked Camel cigarettes back then. How did we know, well every billboard sign in our hometown had men—doctors dressed in white—big as day, holding a lighted Camel cigarette in their hands, the smoke from the tips of their cigarettes circled all the way to the top of the billboard. And to top it all off, the doctors were smiling, and looked very relaxed and happy. If that weren't enough, the caption read: "Have a Camel."

The same pictures were in all the popular magazines. Everywhere you turned, you saw this advertisement. Well, if those doctors told us to have a Camel, Leon and I weren't going to disappoint them. Our next move was to take (steal) a pack of our father's Camels from the carton he kept in the cabinet next to our home line telephone stand. We thought we were clever. We knew how to fool him. We took a pack out of the carton and pushed the other packs from the back forward to make the others in front appear the way he left them.

This winter day, our mother and dad were at the office, so Leon and I lit up. I took a puff and coughed to high Heaven. Leon took a puff and blew it out of his mouth and nose. Smiling like a big shot. "Showoff," I said.

Our day of reckoning had come. Two weeks before Christmas we helped mom wrap packages to take to the post office. On the way,

Leon lit a cigarette. I really didn't like cigarettes that much, but still I lit one up, but didn't take too many puffs. Leon was smoking away. On the way home we opened the windows to let the smoke out, hoping the air would blow smoke off us. We were worried mom would smell it on our clothes while helping her wrap more packages. She didn't say anything. We were in the clear.

When Leon was helping her wrap and tie a large package, mom asked him to hold his finger at the junction where she was to make a bow. She quickly stopped and looked up directly into his eyes, and said, "You've been smoking." Leon stuttered and stammered. "Don't lie to me!" she said, pointing a finger in his face. Mom hated liars. Leon finally said yes. She turned to me. And how about you?" I said, "Not too often." That's the first thing that came out of my mouth. "You know I don't like you kids lying to me. "Yes, mama," we know, shaking.

We learned later from mom that our dad was asking her if she thought he was smoking more than usual. She said no and asked why. He said his cigarettes were going faster than usual but didn't know why. She asked him, "Don't you really know? Your boys have been helping themselves to your cigarettes."

When we were seated at the dinner table the next evening, I was wondering why our mother hadn't served the meal yet. Our dad reached into his pocket and pulled out his cigarettes and placed one in the middle of Leon's empty plate and one on my plate. He said, "I've learned you boys are smoking. I'd rather you not smoke, but if you do, don't smoke behind my back and steal my cigarettes."

In December 1979, I got a call from my friend, Dr. Dewey Garner, the newly elected President of the Kappa Psi Pharmaceutical Fraternity. He and I had talked earlier about the Executive Director position. He wanted to know if I was still interested, and if Dean Ice would approve space for The Central Office. Dr. Garner wanted to move it from California. The Executive Director essentially ran the Fraternity in the International Office, called The Central Office. I had mentioned the possibility of becoming the Executive Director to Dean Ice a couple of months earlier and he thought it would be great for the college and could count towards my Service component, one of the three requirements—Research, Teaching, and Service—of the faculty.

Currently my academic office was on the entire bottom floor of a two-story house, which Medicinal Chemistry occupied. The other faculty had chosen offices on the second floor, which they had chosen much earlier, leaving me with the ground floor.

I told Dr. Garner I would accept the position only if Charmaine could be my administrative assistant. I knew, with all her experience in academia, she would be ideal. Also, I knew I couldn't handle the job without her.

He was pleased to hear my dean was willing to provide the space, and that I was willing to take the position. He had to run Charmaine's position pass the Executive Committee and they'd have to vote on the package deal. First, I was interviewed by Dr. Norm Campbell, one of the Fraternity's great leaders. A day later, in early January 1980, I got word that we were approved, and that the office would be moved from California to Oklahoma City immediately.

Charmaine and I rearranged the space on the main floor, where I would occupy the back area for my office, and we put her desk close to my office where she would be facing the front. There was a small room to the right of her and a lavatory. We got a call from Diane, the secretary that ran the California office. She was so kind and helpful. She developed a list of things that had to be done for the month of January. It was a lifesaver. On this Tuesday morning around eleven our time (nine California time), she had turned the phone over to the movers and the driver told me they were loaded up and had to get another load and would be leaving for Oklahoma City soon after. They'd probably arrive in Oklahoma City early in the morning on Thursday. I asked Diane to wire the money so we could pay the movers. I was shocked to learn that there was no money.

What am I going to do? I called Dr. Garner, our President, and he told me to call the chapters to see if they'd pay their dues early. Charmaine called around with no luck Wednesday around noon, I received a phone call from the movers. They were in OKC and would be delivering our office equipment at five p.m., but for now they were going to get some rest. They didn't have to pick up the other load in California, so they had driven for 22 hours straight from Stockton to OKC.

In shock, again. I asked how much the bill was.

What am I going to do? I had no money.

After much thought, I decided to call our banker in Norman and tell him my situation. He graciously said he'd have a cashier's check ready for me and it would be considered a three-month loan. I rushed to Norman to pick up the check. When I returned, Charmaine and I sat in what was the living room of the home and waited for the moving van. At five o'clock a big yellow truck pulled up in front of our building. It was a cold dreary day, and I felt the same—lifeless, not knowing what to do.

As the movers unloaded the desks, chairs, filing cabinets, electronic equipment and supplies, we directed them where to put each item. When they finished and after I paid them, I told Charmaine, "Let's lock up and go home. We can start tomorrow sorting things out."

The next morning Charmaine and I began organizing the office equipment and supplies and by noon had everything placed where we wanted it. Now we had to go through the filing cabinets and follow the instructions Diane sent for us to begin working with the Chapters and the Executive Committee.

A week later, our Grand Regent, Dr. Dewey Garner, came from Ole Miss to stay several days with us to help arrange things and to get us operational. He was a big help, and we felt more confident after his visit.

CHAPTER 38
Research in Nuclear Pharmacy

In 1977 I was assigned a research facility in a large lab space on the ground floor in one of the science buildings where I continued my research with two graduate students.

Dean Ice's specialty was nuclear pharmacy, and he hired a couple of nuclear faculty to establish it as a new department in the college. He also hired a medicinal chemist, George Parker, who I knew during my postdoc days at Kansas. Now he was working with me in my new research lab.

Four of us were absorbed into Dean Ice's research group. Nuclear chemistry wasn't my specialty, and my interest was in breast cancer. But using our organic chemistry skills, George and I worked two years in my new lab synthesizing organic compounds that would be used in radio imaging after a radioisotope was introduced into them. During one of our research meetings, Ice discussed the radioisotope, Tellurium, chosen to be introduced into our organic compounds (which we called the "cold compounds"), yielding the radioactive isotope (which we called the "hot compounds") to be used in imaging. He had one of the nuclear faculty members, Alan Kirschner, do the calculations and found the isotope produced enough energy to be a good imaging agent. So, they began introducing the isotope into our cold compounds. The animal testing was successful, as reported by the nuclear faculty.

In April 1978 I received the J. P. Baldwin Study/Travel Award for excellence, sponsored by the OU Alumni Association. The students in the College of Pharmacy nominated me for this award. and later I became the first HSC faculty member to receive this award. To be eligible for this award, a nominee must be a member of the faculty and must devote part of his or her time to teaching and advising students. In 1974 and 1976 I received the OU College of Pharmacy outstanding teaching award.

The Baldwin award money of $1000 came at a very opportune time for I was selected by Dean Ice's Research Group to present two papers at the Second International Symposium on Radiopharmaceutical Chemistry, held in Oxford, England. Since the College of Pharmacy did not fund trips for international meetings, the trip would have been too costly for me and Charmaine to go where I would be giving two papers on our new radiopharmaceutical, Tellurium, developed in our college.

Quoted directly from the *hsc Today* publication, volume 2, No. 6, February 1979, *Editor Dee Ann Barbour:*

Using radioactive drugs to scan internal organs for signs of disease is a new development that nuclear pharmacy proponents say is rapidly eliminated the need for exploratory surgery. Its success hinges on developing quality radiopharmaceutical agents. The College of Pharmacy Nuclear team, headed by Dean Rodney D. Ice, has been preforming research to meet this need for new better products. There is only one other research group in the United States testing a new radioactive drug called Tullerium (sic) to gauge its usefulness as a diagnostic agent.

Thanks to Dr. Robert A. Magarian's selection as a Baldwin Award Winner, nuclear pharmacists from around the world heard about the team's research work on Tullerium (sic), a drug so new that Magarian said scientists don't know yet which organs it will work best on.

Magarian is part of a five-man team of pharmacists researching radiopharmaceuticals. The team includes Dr. George Parker, medicinal chemist, Dr. Garabed P. Basmadjian, a radiopharmaceutical chemist and Dr. Alan Kirschner, assistant professor of nuclear pharmacy, and Dean Ice who are involved in the biological testing of the new product.

Magarian's part in the research effort is to conduct what is known as "cold runs" with non-radioactive materials. This is done to perfect the steps for synthesizing new products without wasting the costly radioactive material during the phase of the testing, he said. Once the steps are worked out, Dr. Basmadjian then puts the product through the "hot run" to produce the radioactive drug.

Besides his role with the nuclear team, Magarian conducts research on potential anti-estrogen drugs that might be beneficial in battling breast and uterine cancer.

Magarian and a graduate student have synthesized 20 chemical compounds, and he said one has shown some weak anti-estrogen activity. He is applying for a federal grant to enter another phase in testing the compound's effectiveness on rats, a study he hopes to collaborate on with the Oklahoma Medical Research Foundation.

When I returned from England, Dean Ice told me that some of his colleagues who attended the meeting in Oxford was impressed with our work.

He was excited and had Garo Basmadjian prepare a talk that would be given at the Annual Meeting of the Society of Nuclear Medicine and Molecular Imaging in Seattle in a month. We all flew out together from Oklahoma City. I'll never forget the meeting. Garo went up on stage and presented his paper. I thought he gave an excellent presentation.

When the floor was opened for questions, all hell broke loose. Dean Ice was well known in the field of nuclear medicine and considered one of the top dogs in the country. There were a few other top dogs from Purdue and other major universities in the audience. The one from Purdue challenged our speaker about the suitability of our isotope Tellurium as a good imaging agent. He suggested that we recalculate because his calculations indicated that our isotope could not produce enough energy to be a good imaging agent.

Dean Ice was fuming. After the discussion and during the break, we followed Ice like little ducks behind Daddy Duck, who was tramping out of the meeting room, and went to the wall pay phone—no cell phones then—Ice got hold of Alan Kirschner, who did our calculations. Angrily, he told him to recalculate and call him back immediately. Thirty minutes later we learned he made a mistake, and the challenger was correct; our isotope would not be a good imaging isotope. This made me wonder how was it that the animal testing showed imaging. Something wasn't right.

Ice commanded us to plan on meeting with him at ten o'clock the morning after we returned to the HSC. We wondered what was going to happened to Alan Kirschner, for whom I felt sorry. We knew all hell was going to break loose. As we rolled into Ice's office the next morning, we were shocked. Ice was smiling.

When we settled in, he told us he had a solution to our problem. He went over a step he thought would solve the imaging problem, which, while I wasn't a nuclear expert, I didn't think the step would work. Neither did Garo Basmadjian, who was our radioisotope expert besides Alan Kirschner. After the meeting, I asked Garo if Ice's solution was realistic. He told me it wouldn't work. I then told him I must get back to my breast cancer research. He said that was probably best. It was going to take time to find a new isotope.

Once I went back to my cancer research, Dean Ice turned on me. I couldn't do anything right. He wasn't pleased that I left his research group. While in his group, I could do no wrong. But now my academic life changed. My raises were less, and he became difficult to deal with.

During the year, our new Pharmacy building was being constructed, scheduled to be completed by the end of 1982. I was allowed to look over my new labs and make suggestions to the architects, who knew nothing about chemistry labs.

The Ph.D. degree program in all areas of the basic sciences were approved now that we had research faculty and new research facilities.

In 1982, Dean Ice got crossways with the provost, and he resigned. Associate Dean Shough became interim from 1982-1984.

Annual Baldwin Teaching Awards

CHAPTER 39

The College Moves into Its New Pharmacy Building

In 1983, we moved into our new pharmacy building, named "The Henry D. and Ida Mosier Pharmacy Building," after a couple who donated money to the building and the college as well as monies to OU sports.

Dr. Victor A. Yanchick became our new dean in 1985. He was a Kappa Psi brother and liked having The Central Office in his College of Pharmacy.

I now had three graduate students in medicinal chemistry—Billy Day and May Griffin and Lyn Overacre—who worked in my labs synthesizing my antiestrogenic compounds for study in breast cancer for their Ph.D. dissertations. I wrote an NIH grant on my compounds with a faculty member, Dr. Pento in pharmacology, who tested them for their effectiveness. This grant allowed me to hire two postdocs and a technician. Our testing on the antiestrogens for breast cancer showed some activity, carried out by the pharmacologist and his graduate students, which led to many publications and 10 patents.

The Kappa Psi Central Office also had moved into the new Pharmacy Building along with the other departments and occupied a large office on the lower level.

Charmaine continued as my administrative assistant, supervising The Central Office along with her secretary. My academic office was on the third floor. My daily routine involved working in The Central Office around four or five pm to handle any business that Charmaine had on my desk—phone calls to answer, checks to sign, and seasonal meetings to prepare for.

My major Kappa Psi responsibilities during the year involved organizing an agenda, choosing a site, and reserving rooms for our Annual Executive Committee meeting. The same duties were required of me; reserving rooms for the Executive Committee members attending the Annual National Pharmacy meetings, and reserving space in the exhibit hall for our Kappa Psi Exhibit. Every two years our greatest event, The Grand Council Convention, was held in cities near beaches or other attractive sites, which meant that I had to negotiate a contract with the hotel for 500 sleeping rooms, meeting rooms, special social activities, and negotiate prices for all food and beverage functions. The American Pharmaceutical Association Annual Meeting also required that I make hotel reservations for the Executive Committee, including the exhibit hall.

Charmaine and her secretary stayed busy dealing with all the Kappa Psi Chapters, meeting their needs, keeping records of their membership and their dues. Collecting all their fees and recording them was very time-consuming. Time also was allotted for keeping up with the graduate brothers' chapter dues and keeping up with their current addresses.

In January 1984, our pregnant daughter, Leslie Ann, called us as she rushed to Norman Regional Hospital for delivery. We rushed over to the hospital and into the maternity ward and waited. After giving birth to our first grandchild, Natalie Ann Freude, Leslie was wheeled out of the delivery room and into the hall with Natalie at her side wrapped in a blanket with her face exposed. We approached the gurney with Leslie and Natalie, and before she was wheeled into her room, we got our first look at Natalie, who surprised us by looking up at us—eyes wide open. That thrilled us.

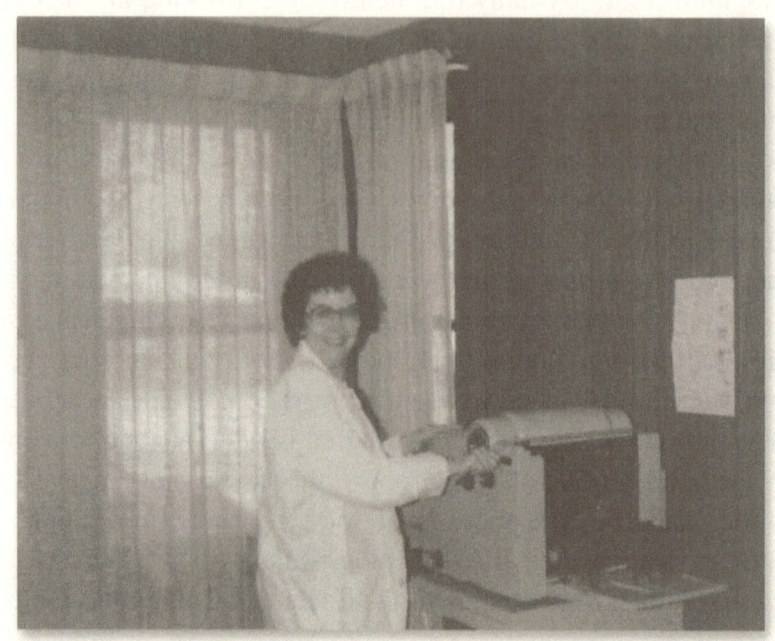

Charmaine in Kappa Psi Central Office

Bob speaking at Kappa Psi GCC

Kappa Psi Exhibit

Bob and Char with Kappa Psi National Officers

Dr. Dewey D. Garner speaking at the GCC

Bob with Kappa Psi Executive Committee

Char and Irish with pseudo cast of MASH

CHAPTER 40
Norman Christmas Day Community Dinner

I nearly gave up on an important dream in 1986. I would have if it weren't for the work of the Holy Spirit.

In late fall, 1985, I was inspired to serve in the community in some way. A few weeks before Thanksgiving, I read an article in the local paper about five churches that took turns in serving Thanksgiving Dinner to the public. I couldn't reach anyone at the church's phone. There was no message on their answering machine about the dinner.

Maybe they were getting too many calls and turned off the answering machine.

When I think back on it, I realize that I could have gone to the church Thanksgiving noon and offered my services but didn't. My lack of resolve shamed me. Usually, I am more proactive. I rationalized not going by telling myself that the church probably had more than enough volunteers anyway, and I could wait until Christmas and call around town to find out who was serving Christmas Dinner and volunteer then. I was off the hook for now.

When December arrived, I called every agency that had anything to do with helping our citizens, and asked who would be serving a free meal on Christmas Day. I was surprised to learn that no one. It was like everything was shut down Christmas Day. Surely there were needy families and homeless persons in our town. I had heard through the grapevine that a restaurant owner served a few meals, but that was it. An employee at one of the agencies told me that it would be quite a task to put on such a dinner and that there was no money available for it. Was she telling me that it couldn't be done? While she didn't come out and say it, I knew from the tone of her voice that she was trying to discourage me. And that annoyed me.

I had remembered hearing someone say: "Find a need and fill it." I thought that this may be my opportunity. But how would I do it? My mind began playing tricks on me: *Maybe you can't pull it off. Didn't that agency person tell you that it was impossible?* Fear had set in, and it was widening a crack in my armor of enthusiasm. Was I going to give in to defeat? That wasn't like me.

Conquering fear starts with a choice to believe God's promises and then taking a step in faith to act on them.

Christmas 1985 came and went, and I still had no plan. Why was I procrastinating? Annoying thoughts assailed me: *Why wasn't I working on a plan for the dinner? Was I hiding from it? How long was I going to wait?* Then I read something that changed me: *One cannot discover new oceans unless one has the courage to lose sight of the shore.* This message spoke to me. My spirits were raised, and I was now beginning to feel a passion for this project.

It's now spring of 1986, and on this sunny afternoon, Char and I were walking through our neighborhood as we do often when the weather is pleasant. We had been walking our route for about twenty minutes when something strange happened to me. A voice in my head "spoke" to me: "you will feed the needy and the homeless on Christmas Day." I looked around. This wasn't one of those Moses-type revelations, was it? I believe psychologists would probably say it was my subconscious mind telling me that because I had been dwelling on thoughts of the dinner for so long. Does the subconscious "speak" to us in sentences? My subconscious had nudged me with "feelings" in the past, but never "talked" to me. This had to be God speaking to me, nudging me. Yes, I believed it was. Now, I had to really get with it. I was on the hook; my back was against the wall. I couldn't disappoint the Holy Spirit, could I? I began pumping myself with the affirmation: *You cannot win if you do not begin.*

As we ambled on in the neighborhood, I told Char what had

happened. She was always very supportive of my projects and this time was no different. She became enthused and volunteered our family— three daughters and son—to help. Maybe I was hoping she would say something negative, to get me off the hook. But I knew the Holy Spirit wouldn't put up with it. She suggested that the Christmas Dinner could be an outreach project from our church. But the congregation was small and so was the church. *Stop your whining and do it,* I thought.

As we continued our walk, I began planning the event in my head. I knew the *when* (Christmas Day) and the *why* (to feed the needy and homeless). What I didn't know was the *where* (where to have it), the *what* (what will it cost?), *who* (who will help?) and the *how* (how many will come).

I realized that the first thing we had to do was determine how many people would come to this dinner. Knowing the number would tell us the size of the place, how many volunteers would be needed, and how much a traditional Christmas dinner would cost per person, since the meal would be free. Could we do it? With the Holy Spirit being with us, we can do it. It was time to make it happen.

Char and I decided to stop along our route at the home of friends, Bob and Evelyn Bibens, who were members of our church, St. Michael's. They, too, became excited after hearing about the plan. They began reciting names of others in our church that would be glad to help. My confidence was building. We sat at the kitchen table and began estimating the number of people we thought would show up to the meal. Evelyn's mother had been a cafeteria supervisor in an out-of-state high school, and she figured how much turkey, dressing, and all the fixings would be needed for one person. Based on several theoretical numbers of attendees, she calculated the costs. We determined that the church could support one hundred people.

Feeling much more confident now, I decided we would move forward and have the dinner, and I'd take the reins and lead the group. We talked with our priest, Fr. Ohl, who was thrilled at the possibility of having the Christmas Day Dinner as the church's outreach project, and so he recommended that I write a proposal for the vestry to review. In the winter of 1986, the Vestry approved my plan, and we began preparing for the 1987 Christmas Day Dinner, which would be sponsored by St. Michael's. We had much to do, and I was glad we had that year to plan.

Our church didn't have a parish hall; consequently, we had many of our social functions in the foyer where there was room for about 12 round tables that sat eight per table. We were counting on the Christmas Spirit to help one hundred people get along in an area that would be overcrowded.

We had another problem. The church's kitchen was too small for us to cook the traditional Christmas meal there. So, I worked out a plan where the ladies agreed to do the cooking and baking, with the provision that the men would do the menial tasks around the church, help them carve the turkeys, and transport the food. Of course, all food items had to be stored in parishioners' homes, since the church didn't have an industrial fridge. As you can imagine, the cooks were very busy the week before Christmas. On Christmas Eve morning a crew of men began setting up the tables and chairs, and with the help of the women dressed the tables in red and green paper tablecloths and decorated the Christmas tree and the foyer. Then they returned to their homes to carve their turkeys and finish their baking. Before leaving the church late Christmas Eve, I checked to make sure nothing was left undone. I felt elated; the place looked like Christmas and had a warm, inviting atmosphere. I had great hopes that this was the beginning of something that God wanted us to continue.

For I was hungry, and you gave me something to eat. I was thirsty and you gave me something to drink. I was a stranger, and you invited me in...Matthew 25:35.

Christmas 1987 had finally arrived. The First Annual Christmas Day Dinner was about to happen. Or was it? I awoke at 4:00 a.m. to one of the worst ice storms recorded in the history of Norman, Oklahoma. When I left the warmth of my home to brave the weather, I was shocked and dismayed at the horrible winter scene I was witnessing. The earth was covered with ice and broken tree branches, and telephone lines were sagging at the weight of the ice, reminding me of a slumped back of an old plough horse. Sleet pelted my face as I trekked to my car. After twenty minutes of scraping, I was able to open the driver's side door and turn on the heater blower to full speed. It took me another ten minutes to clean the windshield. I could still see sheets of sleet streaming in front of the streetlamp on the corner. Before sliding in behind the steering wheel, I looked up to the Heavens and asked God if this were a test. I told Him if it were, I prayed that He was with me because now, I had enough on my plate. After all, wasn't I doing this for Him?

I slowly backed out of the driveway, sliding into the street, doing a 180. I finally got the car turned in the right direction and eased on the accelerator to inch along for the next two blocks to the stoplight at Main Street where I made a left turn without stopping, and gradually entered the center lane. As I motored on, an eerie feeling came over me. It was quiet, graveyard quiet. No humans in sight. No cars were on the road. It was five o'clock. The scene was surreal. I felt like I was in a dream. For a moment, I felt all alone and wondered if the Rapture had occurred. *Was I left behind?* Again, I talked to God: "Something's not right here. I thought I had already earned enough brownie points to be zoomed up?" No answer. *Well, maybe it wasn't the Rapture after all,* I thought. I continued creeping along over the icy roads. It took me twenty minutes more to make it to the church. Finally, we were going to have our free Christmas Dinner. Or were we? *Would this weather foil our attempts?* I banished the thought.

Not to worry. It was in His hands now.

As I slid into the parking lot, I noticed the lights were on inside the church. This gave me a sense of relief, knowing that my loyal friend and sidekick, Howard Moore, was already there. When I entered the building, I learned he had been there since 4:00 a.m. He was connecting the red electrical cords into the ten borrowed roasting ovens—like grandma used to use—lined along two walls in a series like boxcars in a train. We began filling the roasters with water that would heat the food when it came.

At eight o'clock, the turkey, dressing, mashed potatoes, gravy and green beans had arrived and were placed into the roasters. At nine, there was a Christmas Morning Service. We had to make a path between the tables so the worshippers could get into the nave. As I watched for them, I noticed that the sleet hadn't let up. Only a few worshippers came, complaining mightily about the bad weather and how it took

187

them three times as long to get here. Now, that wasn't what I wanted to hear. After the service, we turned our attention back to the dinner. With a cup of coffee in hand, I looked over the area and was extremely proud of what everyone had done.

By ten-thirty, the twenty-four volunteers—including my wife and four children—were ready. The gifts, pies, cakes, rolls and cranberry sauce were also in place. The Dinner was scheduled for 11:00 a.m. to 2:00 p.m. It was now time to send the borrowed school bus out on the town to collect the people. Weeks before, we had passed out fliers at all the agencies and a brief article about St. Michael's free Christmas Day Dinner appeared in the local paper. My son-in-law was the driver of the bus, and he expressed grave concern about the ice and some felled trees across the roads. I told him to be safe, but I wanted him to try and make it to the designated routes.

Close to eleven o'clock, all the twenty-four volunteers waited by the double doors for the school bus's return. At 11:10 it arrived. We waited with great anticipation. The bus doors opened. Our hearts sank. We were in shock. One young man in his twenties stepped off the bus. No one said a thing. When the young man came in, he was greeted by a legion of smiling faces, guided to the serving table, where the workers took their places. This young man must have thought he was the Maharaja of one of the Indian states, with all the attention, food, and finally being seated at one of the twelve empty tables.

My son-in-law came rushing into the church out of breath. The school bus had caught fire, but thankfully, he was able to extinguish it. He wanted to know what he should do. I told him to pull the bus round to the side of the church and park it. I couldn't help but wonder if anything else was going to happen. Hadn't we had enough testing?

Several volunteers wanted to know what we were going to do. Without answering, I recruited four other drivers besides myself to go out on the icy roads and pick up the people. We left in a caravan. The roads were treacherous, but the sleet had stopped. We had to detour around several fallen trees. When we made it back to the church, I counted ten people getting out of the cars. As we entered the church, I counted ten more people at the tables eating Christmas Dinner, smiling and talking with the volunteers. We didn't reach our expected one hundred guests, but twenty was a miracle. It was a delight to see the smiles on the faces of the children. Since we had counted on more children, those present received three or four toys, candy, scarves and gloves.

Close to 2:00 p.m. many of the church members gathered around me, wondering what I thought about the dinner. Most were pleased, but some wondered if it was worth it and asked if I was going to do it again. From the tone of their voices, I could tell that they were discouraged with the turnout, but they were overlooking the weather.

Stay in faith and God will get you to where you need to be.

I didn't answer them at first, because I was looking at a couple with two children seated at a table close to the wall. The boy and girl had big smiles on their faces, playing with their new toys. My heart wrenched when I saw tears in the mother's eyes.

I pointed to the family and asked my churchgoers if they noticed the smiles on the faces of that family. Then I revealed to the volunteers what that father had told me earlier: "Sir," he said, "If it wasn't for this church, my family wouldn't have Christmas. I lost my job two weeks ago." I went on to tell the volunteers that that family's situation is reason enough for us to continue having our Christmas Day Dinner, and that I was sure there would be others in that situation every Christmas.

We increased our advertising for the Second Annual Christmas Day Dinner, and one hundred people showed up. Thank God the weather cooperated. Since it appeared we were growing and our church couldn't hold any larger number of people, a decision had to be made about moving to another venue. I felt fortunate that the Norman High School cafeteria was available to rent for the Third Annual Christmas Day Dinner. We doubled our attendance and saw a need to offer rides to the dinner and make deliveries to shut-ins when preparing for the Fourth Annual Dinner. Also, deliveries to the clients of Meals-on-Wheels were taken on, as well as a Santa Claus. The attendance reached four hundred.

After the Fourth Annual Dinner, we found ourselves faced with two problems: we needed more volunteers and more money. Hence, I decided that the dinner had to become a community event—but it would still be sponsored by St. Michael's Episcopal Church—and donations would be requested. Hence, we published articles in the local paper and distributed fliers to all agencies and posted them in all businesses. I added the names: "Norman" and "Community" to the title so that the Fifth Annual Dinner became known as the Norman Christmas Day Community Dinner, and was now supported by banks, businesses, and private donations. We stressed in our advertising that the dinner was FREE and open to everyone—anyone who wanted to have a meal and spend some time with others during Christmas Day. I now assumed the title of Director of the dinner.

A carpenter friend and I built six large double-sided signs that were painted with the name of the dinner, its location, serving time, and our motto: *No one should eat alone on Christmas Day*. During the years the motto got interchanged with: *No one should be alone on Christmas Day*, so we've accepted both. These signs were placed at various locations in the city.

The dinner that fifth year attracted more students and faculty from the University of Oklahoma, senior citizens, and visitors staying in local motels, besides the needy and homeless. Six hundred showed up. We were blessed with more volunteers than needed. Norman has wonderful people who love to help those in need. Many tell me that working the dinner is rewarding and spiritual to them. Some call me as early as October for fear that they won't get on the list to participate.

We received donations of pies, cakes, and Poinsettias for the tables every year. Sometimes we're surprised with boxes of candies from companies and trays of cupcakes. People in the community deliver children's toys, knitted scarves, gloves, and gifts for all ages. We have items for adults, also.

On Christmas Eve '09, Oklahoma was hit with a blizzard. Most of the state closed, even the interstates. We had just finished our preparations for the Christmas Dinner at the Norman High School when it hit. I was the last to leave, and nearly didn't make it home. Thoughts of our first dinner twenty-three years earlier crossed my mind. That evening, all closures of businesses, social functions, parties, and churches streamed across the bottom of our TVs. I got calls from volunteers asking if we were going to have the dinner. I told them we were, even if only a few came. Christmas morning, I stood by the large windows of the high school commons facing Main Street, watching. Here they came, singles, couples, and groups trekking through the foot of snow. The scene brought tears to my eyes. Nothing was going to keep them from celebrating this day. We fed 400.

In 1987, we had twenty-four volunteers, and now we used two hundred. We fed 20 people then and in 2010 we fed 1600.

Christmas Day 2011 was the Twenty-Fifth Anniversary of the Norman Christmas Day Community Dinner, and we were expecting the same number, maybe more.

Now who was it that told me this project couldn't be done?

Never, ever give up on your dream. I'm glad I didn't.

Over the years, I have been asked by the media why I'm doing the dinner. First, I told them that it was "we" and not "I" that made the dinner possible because it took two hundred volunteers and many donors to accomplish it, and secondly, I told them we were doing the work of the Lord. But now I have a new message for them, which I believe the Lord, Jesus Christ, revealed to me. I will now tell the reporters that the Christmas Dinner has taught me a valuable lesson: *When you bring joy to others, joy fills your life.* I believe Booker T. Washington had discovered this long before me when he wrote: *The only thing worth living for is the lifting up of our fellow man.*

God bless!

*Bob with Bobby D.
working the Christmas
Dinner*

Paula in charge of the dessert section

CHAPTER 41
My Retirement and Our 50th Wedding Anniversary

In June 1995, I submitted my letter of intent to retire as of June 30, 1996, to give the dean a year to appoint a search committee to seek applicants to interview for my position. I began closing my labs, writing articles of our work for publication, and the final reports on our research to submit to the National Cancer Institute. My last Ph.D. student had finished her research and requirements for her dissertation and was heading to Kansas for a postdoc position with one of my former masters student, Dr. John Stobaugh.

During the remaining days of this last year on the faculty, something stimulating began happening to me in the mornings as Char and I drove together to work. I began receiving visions of different scenes and ideas. At first, I'd just let them pass, but they were persistent. Eventually, I couldn't help but wonder if someone was telling me to write these ideas down.

I thought long and hard about these visions. I wondered if closing my labs and having completed all articles for publication, had removed the pressure I was under, and now I was open to ideas that could flow easily through me? I started writing the ideas down, but they didn't make much sense. So, I didn't do much with them in 1995 and early 1996.

In June 1996, the College of Pharmacy held a retirement party for me on a Friday evening, which took place on the top floor of the Petroleum Club in OKC, where one could look out over the City. It was beautiful. Many of the faculty, my relatives from out of town, and my Kappa Psi Executive Committee brothers were in attendance. I was honored that they all came.

There were speeches and gifts. One faculty member gave me one of the T-shirts that the students in my Med Chem class had made with 10 funny remarks on the back. You've probably guessed, they weren't meant to be complimentary, but funny, and you'd be right. From the Executive Committee. Brother Grossomanides presented me with a beautiful Mont Blanc fountain pen on behalf of the Fraternity. Dr. Dewey Garner, Chairman of the Department of Pharmacy Administration at Ole Miss, my Alma Mater, presented me with a beautiful Ole Miss sweatshirt. I also was pleased to receive the beautiful University Chair for retiring faculty from the college.

When it came my time to speak, I got up and went to the podium that was positioned close by my table. Little did I know that my brother, Dr. Edward Magarian, a Medicinal Chemistry professor from North Dakota State University, would get up and push me aside and say, "What's with you people? I'm tired of hearing all the good things you've said about this guy," pointing at me. "You don't know him. He and my older brother Leon tried to hang me when I was only 7 years old." That brought the house down. He went on to say, "My brother Bob here, this guy here," he said pointing, again, "told my older brother, 'We better not hang him, mom wouldn't like it.'" And that brought the house down again. "Can you believe he said, 'Mom wouldn't like it?' I certainly wouldn't have liked it." Some of the faculty were on their feet clapping. I guessed they got their thrill for the night. Ed finally ended with something nice to say about me.

When it came my time to speak, I stole a few lines from Martin Luther King's "*I got a Dream*" speech, I raised my hands in the air and shouted, "Free at last! Free at last! Thank God Almighty, I'm free at last!" which brought much laughter and was a big hit with the faculty. I thanked everyone for coming and then introduced Charmaine, our children, and all our relatives that came from out of town, and my brothers on the Executive Committee of Kappa Psi. My speech was short dealing with a brief review of my years with the college and thanking everyone for their support.

Dean Yanchick couldn't make it to my retirement party due to his wife's battle with cancer. Associate Dean Richard Shough spoke after me to thank me for all I did for the college.

Interestingly, Dean Yanchick also retired at the end of the 1996 school year to take the deanship at the School of Pharmacy, Virginia Commonwealth University, in Richmond, Virginia.

That weekend the Executive Committee members spent a full day at our home after visiting the OKC bombing memorial that Saturday morning. We spent most of the day in the garage, where I had set up a long table with chairs and fans. We had plenty of goodies to eat and drink and Char had a retirement cake for the occasion. It was a wonderful, memorial time I had with my brothers of the Executive Committee.

For the next four years, Char and I were allowed to continue in The Central Office with our secretary, even though I was retired. But in 2000 Char and I decided it was time to give it up after 20 and ½ years. In addition, we were receiving hints from the dean's office that our space was needed by the college, which we found out later it wasn't. I believe the Assistant Dean wanted us out.

But before we even thought about packing, we had another big event we were attending to, and that was our 50th Wedding Anniversary, June 24, 2000.

Plans were underway to have a great celebration in the large, open area of dining rooms on the OU campus, to be held on our anniversary, which fell on a Saturday evening. University Catering was hired to prepare an outstanding meal, drinks, a large cake, and great desserts. I had arranged for the students who play the string instruments in the University orchestra to play all evening, especially as the guests were arriving.

Invitations were sent to friends and relatives locally and out of town. Everyone responded favorably. All came. We were so pleased and happy that our large family came from all over. There were speeches, toasts, and singing. I believe the highlight of the evening occurred during dancing. Everyone had a grand time, and we were so blessed to have everyone with us on our big day.

Bob speaking at his Pharmacy Retirement party

Ed & Sandy at Bob's retirement party

Celebrating Bob's retirement

Bob and Char's 50th Wedding Anniversary

Celebrating Bob & Char's 50th Wedding Anniversary

CHAPTER 42
My Writing Career

This last day of June 2000, was the day the movers came to the college around seven, to move the Kappa Psi furniture out of The Central Office to be shipped to the School of Pharmacy in Weatherford, OK, 90 miles west of Oklahoma City, where Dr. Scott Long, a brother and Pharmacology faculty member, became the new Executive Director.

It was a sad day for Charmaine and me. We thought about the many happy memories we developed over twenty years working with so many outstanding brothers in the Fraternity: Undergraduate and graduate members, Deans, Faculty, Chairs of Departments, Pharmaceutical Industry leaders, and many leaders in Pharmacy organizations. They would be sorely missed.

Now Char and I would have to redirect our time doing other things, but it would take some time to get used to not being involved with the Fraternity. We did some traveling, visited relatives, and worked more at our church—preparing and distributing Thanksgiving baskets and continuing with the Norman Christmas Dinner—spent two days a week at Barnes and Nobles bookstore. Went to the Y three days a week and walked in our neighborhood.

Now that I was on my own time, I became very serious about writing. I read books on writing fiction. Two of my favorites are: J. Madison Davis,' Novelist's *Essential Guide to Plotting* and Stephen Wilber's, *Keys to Great Writing*.

I attended workshops held at a local hotel and supervised by Dr. J Madison Davis, Endowed Professor in the Journalism Department at OU. He invited many well-known writers from whom I picked up pointers on writing fiction.

During one of the workshops, an old friend of mine, Robert Ferrier, was one of the speakers. I knew Robert as head of the department that reviewed my research grants on the Norman campus before we moved to the HSC.

After his presentation, he waved for me to come forward. He invited me to lunch to catch up on what I have been doing. At the lunch, he asked what genre I was writing in. At the time it was a medical thriller. I asked if he could help me with my writing. He was pleased that I asked, and we planned on lunch twice a month during which time we would work on my writing. He found my writing stiff and instructed me to practice writing whatever came to my mind— streams of consciousness. This I did but it took me over a month to please him, and I still had to loosen up more. Robert told me that I had to work at getting out of the scientific mode of writing that I was used to. He also taught me about principles in writing fiction. During his continued "bashing" of me about my stiff writing, I decided that I needed to copy some author's work to get the real feel of writing fiction. One of my favorite authors was Sidney Sheldon. I enjoyed *Doomsday Conspiracy* and decided to copy it from cover to cover. I bought a ream of legal pads and began writing from the first Chapter to the end of the last Chapter. I started writing slowly to get the feel of the flow in Sheldon's writing and his choice of words. For me, feeling is everything. Also, I paid close attention to the structure of the novel, and how he wrote his dialogue. I concentrated on all the elements of fiction that I knew but paid special attention to the flow of his words. By the time I got half-way through the novel, I felt like I was the protagonist moving through each subsequent scene in the remaining chapters. When I finished copying the novel, I felt I now had some idea how to write fiction, and the stiffness began leaving me. This took me two weeks of writing every day, which produced a stack of legal pads on my desk. Robert felt I had improved, even though I never told him what I had done. I never told anyone at the time.

I decided I was now ready to write my first medical thriller. I got an idea about a molecular biologist being in a horrific life-threating situation but didn't know to get him out of it. Plotting was new to me, and I didn't do a very good job. I wrote events that I thought would test the biologist to see how he would respond, but in doing so, I wrote myself into a corner, and I struggled to find my way out. I probably wrote an equivalent of three books before I felt I got the story right. The valuable lesson I learned is: a writer needs to spend at least three months plotting his sequence of events, making sure that they follow in a cause-and-effect relationship before writing one word. *The Watchman*, a medical thriller, became my first novel.

After the publication of my first novel, *The Watchman*, I did my first book signing at Borders Bookstore in Norman. The experience was rewarding, and the event introduced me into the authors world. Then I tried to schedule a signing at the local Barnes and Noble bookstore, but since I wasn't a well-known author and had self-published my book, they didn't welcome me. They did, however, agree to handle my book.

After that I got the idea of doing a presentation and book signing on *The Watchman* at the famous Square Books in Oxford, Mississippi, where John Grisham, Larry Brown, Willie Morris, and Barry Hannah made presentations and signed their books. My thought was to impress on Square Books that I was an alumnus of Ole Miss, got three degrees from there. lived in Oxford for ten years and two of our children were born in Oxford. I really laid it on. The nice lady I talked to stated she'd display my book in the store, set a date for my presentation and would order my books. Charmaine and I notified all our Ole Miss friends and the College of Pharmacy faculty about the event. Square Books advertised the event in the local paper, the Oxford Eagle.

Several days before the event, Charmaine and I had planned to stay at one of the local motels with our old friends, Jimmy and Anna Ray Gassaway, and Joe and Doris Allen, who were our neighbors when we first enrolled in 1954. They came not only for our reunion but to attend my book signing.

The day before the event, Charmaine and I visited Square Books on the square across from the historic courthouse. I was pleased to see The Watchman on display on a table close to the door. I meet with the lady, and all was set for the next day. The event will take place at Off Square Books at 5:30 pm and scheduled to last about two hours. The sheet she gave me showed 45 minutes for my talk and reading, and 30 minutes for questions, and an hour to sign my books.

Before strolling a few doors east of the main store to Off Square Bookstore, a satellite store, which was in New's Drug Store. where I had copied prescriptions in the '50s and '60s, I couldn't resist taking a picture of Char close to the historic Courthouse, where in the 1996 movie of John Grisham's novel *A Time to Kill*, the courthouse was used by Matthew McConaughey an untested attorney to defend the black man who avenged his daughter's brutal rape by shooting the bigoted men responsible for the crime.

Arriving at Off Square Books, I took a picture of Char at the store front with its large windows and well-organized book displays. We entered and found the place enchanting. The store was a large facility and had no resemblance to what I remembered. The place was filled with a nice sitting area for reading and relaxing. Books filled both walls as far into the store as one could see. I was impressed and honored to be able to give a talk in such a place. About three dozen chairs had already been arranged in place like a small classroom,

That evening the Gassaways, Allens and Char and I had a nice two-hour meal in one of the local restaurants on the Square. It was a rare treat to be with old friends reliving the past and learning about their families and careers.

The day I had been waiting for had arrived and I admit I was a little uptight. I wondered how many would come to hear an unknown author. I was prepared and had no problem speaking before groups, not after being a former professor for 30 years, I felt confident. I was hoping that some of the University faculty would show up. We were told to arrive early to set up and be available to meet the guests as they arrived. We arrived at the site around four-thirty pm. The personnel of Square Books had set my books on a counter with a register at one end. The plan was to have the guests buy the book and then come to me for signing. Up front was a table covered with a white tablecloth and a pail of ice with wine bottles and some snacks, cups and napkins on the side. In the middle of the room against the wall close to the chairs setup in classroom style was a table and chair for my book signing. I was impressed with the arrangement and how nicely the personnel treated me and Char. The Allens came with us, but the Gassaways had to leave earlier for another commitment.

Dr. Dewey Garner and his sweet wife, Barbara, and Dr. Ron Borne, from the College of Pharmacy were the first to arrive. I've written about brother Garner and a little about Ron Borne who was at Kansas when I was there. Ron and I became very close friends and he, too, became a writer. We enjoyed our talks about writing.

The Dean of the College of Pharmacy Barbara Wells, and her husband, Richard arrived next and joined our group. Several minutes later I began welcoming everyone. John Leslie, the owner of Leslie's Pharmacy, and the current mayor, showed up with his wife. I had known John for years and was honored to see him again. I greeted many others from the community and from the University and when it came time for my presentation, I figured about 40 people were in attendance.

To start the program, Dr. Garner introduced me and told everyone about my time at the University, our friendship and my accomplishments.

To start off I read the synopsis and first chapter of *The Watchman*. Then I talked about writing, the elements of fiction, how to develop characters, and about one of my favorite subjects, plotting, the structure of a novel, and about story.

When finished, I opened the floor for questions. I was asked where I got my idea for The Watchman, another asked if I used the computer, or did I write in a notebook, do I write every day, what time of day do I write, and a few questions about characterization and dialogue.

When finished, one of the Square Books persons instructed the people, "You can purchase Dr. Magarian's book at the counter and then move to the table where he will be happy to sign your book."

The attendees rose and went to the counter to purchase a book. Many took advantage of the wine and snacks. I signed dozens of books. When finished, I mingled with the crowd and was pleased to hear many enjoyed my talk. The Chairman of the Medicinal Chemistry Department, Steve Cutler, and Professor Chris McCurdy slipped into the back of the room during my presentation and waited. Cutler informed me that Char and I and the Allens were invited to a College of Pharmacy dinner along with the Dean and her husband and all the faculty in attendance planned in my honor. The dinner was held in one of the top-ranked restaurants on the Square and was fabulous. It felt good to be back in Oxford with all my friends. I have never forgotten their graciousness shown to me and Charmaine.

While writing my second novel, *72 Hours*, I felt the need for some special instructions. Every May OWFI (Oklahoma Writers Federation Incorporated) held a statewide writers conference in OKC. Robert Ferrier and I attended and in the registration packet was a flyer from Carolyn Wall, author and teacher, who lived in OKC. The flyer described classes she held in her home once a week. So, I joined up. There were six of us. I really enjoyed the classes, but felt I needed more one-on-one instruction. I didn't want to hog class time with so many questions I wanted to ask. During the coffee break, I asked Carolyn if she held private lessons, that I felt I needed more supervision. She did and for the next two years we met in her kitchen every Thursday morning for two hours. She had coffee ready.

We went through most of my *72 Hours* chapter-by-chapter and Carolyn taught me about the beginning, middle, and ending of a novel. I learned how conflict was essential to have a story and plotting was important. I believe the Lord sent me to her because she is a jewel of a teacher and such a kind person. She gave me confidence and I'm forever grateful.

After *72 Hours*, I switched genres into detective mystery. I had always liked mystery and thought it was what I should be doing. So, I began with my third novel, *You'll Never See Me Again, A Crime to Remember."* I spent three months plotting before I wrote a word in this novel. Plotting became one of my favorite tasks and I felt it was so important that time should be spent making sure all the sequence of events flowed through cause and effect.

I wondered if spending that much time plotting was because I was slow or trying to be a perfectionist. I enrolled in one of James Patterson's virtual classes on writing. To my surprise, he stated that he spent three months plotting his novels before he wrote a word. That gave me a boost in my confidence.

I broke up my writing time with our family get-togethers and having our cookouts. In 2012 we learned that our granddaughter Natalie Stephens was pregnant, and in April 2013 gave birth to our lovely great-granddaughter, Blakely Ann Stephens.

After my third novel, I wrote two more detective mysteries with co-author detectives-*The Tongue Collector,* and *Forever Young*—and have written two essays. Writing is a lonely vocation and requires support, which I received from my lovely wife, Charmaine.

Bob signing The Watchman at Borders Bookstore

Char standing across from the famous Oxford Courthouse

*Bob & Char in front of
Off Square Bookstore*

Bob and Char with the Allens and Gassaways

Bob & Char sitting in the waiting area
before his presentation

Bob's presentation

Bob signing books

Bob & Charmaine with Dr. Joseph Sam

College of Pharmacy Dinner to honor Bob

CHAPTER 43

In Remembrance of Our Only Son: Robert Dwight

Monday, August 07, 2017, at eight in the evening I got a call from Angela, our daughter-in-law, who was still at her office, waiting on our son, Bob, to pick her up. She hadn't been able to reach him. Bob was her business manager, and he worked in their home office in east Norman and usually picked Angela up after she was through for the day in her counseling office in the west end of town. She asked if I could take her home.

I had a bad feeling driving over to her. After we left her office, I told her to call 911 and have them meet us at their home in case Bob was unconscious. There were times he fainted due to lack of magnesium.

When we arrived, we rushed into the house and found Bob bent over his desk with his head resting on the desk with the right side of his face exposed. I rubbed his arms and checked his face. He was as white as a sheet and cold.

Angela screamed, "He's dead!"

I laid my head, face down, on his and hugged him as the EMTs were at the door. I kissed him on his head and face before they could get into the room.

Our only son, I thought. Why, Bob, why?

They asked us to step out.

Angela and I were in shock. We stepped out the office door, but

I stopped and turned to watch them. All I could think of is—poor Charmaine. I had to call her. The EMT personnel came out of his office as I stepped aside, told us that Bob had passed and they were sorry, there was nothing they could do. They were so kind.

The police arrived.

I wanted to go back into Bob's office to be with him, but the officer standing at the door told me that she had to seal the area to protect Bob until they could determine what had happened to him. I could tell her but decided not to.

I was certain he had cardiac arrest, and no one was with him to help. He had a history of fainting and did so several times. Once in his home kitchen when Angela had to call 911 and then she called me. I went to the hospital to be with him and learned he was low on magnesium and was given an I.V.

Now Angela's home was filled with a half-dozen police officers and the one in charge was interviewing Angela.

I don't know who called our girls, but they rushed to our home to be with their mother. I called Charmaine and told her the bad news. We had lost our only son, Bob D. Magarian at the age of 55 years. No child should go before his/her parents. I felt I should be the one leaving this earth before him.

I got the feeling that the officer in charge was trying to determine if anyone had intentionally harmed Bob. I presumed that was his modus operandi. Jimmy Fletcher, a Norman Police Officer and friend, heard the news in his patrol car and came to the house. It was comforting to see him. He was so kind, talked with us and then to the chief and told him we were good people.

Since they couldn't get hold of Bob's cardiologist or primary care physician, the ME in Oklahoma City was contacted, and the personnel came for Bob's body. When they brought him out in a black bag on a gurney, I asked the attendant if he'd open the bag so we could have one last goodbye. He was so kind and did so with warmth in his eyes. Once the bag was unzipped, he stepped back. Bob's head was exposed, I hugged him, laid my head on his, gave him one last kiss, and said goodbye. Angela bent down and kissed Bob, too. My heart was heavy watching the ME personnel zip the bag up and wheel Bob out to the hearse. He was eventually released to Havenbrook Funeral Home.

The police officers were now leaving, and someone had brought Mary Peterson, Angela's mother, to the house.

Time for me to leave.

Back home, I immediately went to Charmaine, who was in her chair with very sad, red eyes. I knelt in front of her, and we hugged, and I remember her saying, "We lost our only son." Our daughters and granddaughter were all with us, shedding tears of sadness.

The next day I got a call from our primary care physician, Dr. Tom Merrill. When I answered the call, he said, "Bob, what in the world happened?"

I said, "I don't know. I think he might have had cardiac arrest, and no one was there to help him." Dr. Merrill also thought that was a possibility.

Our out-of-town families were notified, and once we learned Angela was having Bob's funeral service at Bethel Baptist Church on the 14th of August, we relayed the dates to them. She was having Bob cremated.

My brother Ed and Sandy and son Kevin and family from Fargo, Melanie, our niece from St. Louis, Charmaine's sister Jeannie and husband Tony, and Scott and Lupe Waldrup from Illinois, came, which gave us strength, to have them with us. Many wonderful friends from our church, St. Michael's, and friends close to Paula and to us, brought us food and warm support.

I wrote a tribute to Bob but couldn't read it. I knew my emotions would get to me and I wouldn't be able to finish. So, I had the minister read my tribute to our only son.

To our son Bobby D.

The Lord took our son, Bob Dwight Magarian, from us on Monday, August 07, 2017. He made a mistake, he was supposed to take me, his father. I never believed the Lord made mistakes, but he did in this case. No child should precede his parents in death. Bob had so many more years to live with his wonderful wife, Angela. I was 32 when our son was born to Charmaine and me. At 55 he should have had those years (I'm 87, 32 years older than Bob) to live on. I'm sorry,

Bob, that I couldn't give them to you. If the Lord asked, I would have gladly given them to you. You were so precious and loving, with such kindness in your heart.

Bob, you made people laugh and be comfortable in your presence. My son, I'm proud to say as your father that you had learned the two most important Commandments that Christ had taught us, on which hang all the law and prophets: To love thy God with all thy heart and with all thy soul and all thy might, and the second is like unto it: Thou shalt love thy neighbor as thy self. You lived according to these Commandments. Mom and I are so proud of you. You will live on with us every minute of the day. Please, Lord, take good care of our son, Bob. Amen.

From Bob's sister, Leslie:

Bob never met a stranger, a kind generous brother/uncle. Made us laugh with his sense of humor and jokes. Dedicated to his family and church. Always there for us when we needed help or a listening ear.

From Bob's sister, Cindy:

Bob was the kindest, gentlest person a sister could ever ask for. He would give the shirt off his back even if it was the last one he owned.

I never saw him happier the day he fell in love with his soulmate and wife, Angela. He loved her with all his heart, and it showed. Bob, know that we will take great care of her for you.

While the church was packed with loved ones and friends, Charmaine and I were the last ones to stand by Bob's casket. Our hearts were heavy as we viewed our son for the last time. We felt numb. First Charmaine leaned over and kissed him. When I leaned down to kiss him goodbye, it felt like someone ripped my heart out. He was going to be wheeled away and cremated and gone from us forever. Our consolation was: he would be with our Lord and Savior, Jesus Christ, and our family in heaven.

While we were having lunch at the church, I stepped out to go to the bathroom and a young man stopped me and said, "Mr. Magarian, I want you to know that at work we really liked Bob. He was helpful and always making us laugh. We'll miss him." I thanked him and told him that was very kind of him to tell me that about Bob. He smiled and left, and I felt a little better.

A couple days later, our out-of-town family left for their homes. Charmaine and were now alone with our thoughts. We felt the eeriness of being alone. We tried but it was difficult to overcome our sadness. We thought about the time when Bob was born and how loving and kind he was growing up. He never gave us any problems.

Why, Lord? Our only son. What did we do, or not do?

CHAPTER 44

More Heartbreak in The Magarian Family

In September, a little over a month after Bobby D. had passed, and we were still trying to cope with the loss of our only son, our oldest daughter, Paula Marie, developed severe headaches. She thought it was from her grief over the loss of her brother. She celebrated her birthday on September 25, turned sixty-one, and soon after, the headaches grew worse. She called me on the Saturday evening after her birthday complaining of severe headaches. I went to her home and brought her to our home. She slept on one couch in our den and I on the other, to watch her during the night.

Early Sunday morning we went to the ER at Norman Regional Hospital. After being in triage, they placed us in one of the examining rooms and connected Paula up to all the equipment around the bed. Her blood pressure was high, heart racing and the severe headaches persisted. The middle-aged lady doctor finally came in and asked if Paula had migraines. She stood to one side at the foot of the bed the whole time and never came to Paula's side to talk directly to her or examine her. I didn't like her bedside manner and thought she seemed rather shallow in her knowledge. She asked questions that didn't make much sense and never once touched Paula. She was convinced it was migraine and suggested we go to a pharmacy and purchase pseudoephedrine, an over-the-counter med. I nearly jumped out of my chair to strangle her.

Where did she receive her medical training? I thought.

The doc didn't know pseudoephedrine was a vasoconstrictor that raises blood pressure. Paula's blood pressure was already sky high. We left and I told Paula the doctor didn't know what she was talking about. We weren't getting any pseudoephedrine. Very early the next morning, a Monday, I called our primary care doctor's office, and we got in immediately.

During his questioning and examining Paula, she couldn't remember what day it was or who was the President, He had her stand, and she had no balance. He said he was calling the hospital for them to run a CT scan. We left his office and reported to the hospital. They took us in right away, placed Paula in an ER examining room, prepared her, and the techs came to wheel her out of the room as I sat next to the bed and waited. Forty minutes later, they wheeled her back into the room and made her comfortable in the bed. Twenty minutes later, a doctor came in and explained that they noticed a brain tumor in Paula, and they were admitting her. Once they got Paula into a room, and began giving her an I.V., I went for her mother. We sat with her and waited for more information. We got word out to family, and everyone came. In the meantime, a spinal neurosurgeon told us that they'd have to do surgery. This scared me. What were his qualifications and doing brain surgery at a local hospital? I don't think so. We discussed it with Paula, but we didn't know what to do. Fortunately, Paula's son, David Blanton, and wife, Megan, came to be with us. Megan was a nurse at Children's hospital in the Health Sciences Center in Oklahoma City. Both David and Megan told us not to allow these people here to touch her.

Megan had talked to her MD Chief of Staff, who contacted Dr. Michael Sughrue, a famous neurosurgeon, who said he would take Paula, but we had to wait for a bed to open in the University Hospital.

What a blessing! Thank God!

We called our primary care doctor and told him the story. He agreed to no surgery locally. He called the local neurosurgeon and told him Paula would be going to University Hospital in Oklahoma City. Paula was then placed in another room on another floor as a holdover. They took very good care of her while she waited for the transfer. The local neurosurgeon came in and checked her over. He was very nice and as he left, I walked out with him and asked what he'd do if he did the surgery. He said he would take half the tumor out and then do radiation.

A death sentence for sure! I thought. *Thank God, we're leaving!*

As I contemplated this difficult situation, I wondered why in the world this hospital would allow such a doctor to do brain surgery.

After a few days, Paula was transported to University Hospital in Oklahoma City. It took several days to prepare her for surgery. Dr. Sughrue liked his patients awake and able to talk. His staff trained Paula for the surgery. While the training was going on, our attorney's clerk came to Paula's room for us to sign papers to give me power of attorney, because Paula wanted me to take charge, and she didn't want to handle anything.

The day of surgery. we all gathered around Paula as she lay on a gurney ready to go into the surgical suite. We gave her a kiss and held her hand and said we'd be waiting for her to come out. She looked a little scared, which she confirmed later.

The family sat in the waiting room during the surgery and to our surprise, Paula's dear friends, Chuck and Gail Pendley, came from Norman to be with us. After a couple of hours, the doctor came in and told us the bad news. The tumor was a glioblastoma. One of the deadliest. Life expectancy 15 months. But he got it all out.

Will it return?

Tears flowed from our eyes. Another trip into the dream world for her mother and me. This couldn't be happening to us again. We all sat, numb, and couldn't speak. Tears flowed from our eves. We weren't over the loss of our son, and now a battle to fight for the life of our oldest daughter.

Lord, we can't lose another one of our children.

While recuperating in her room, Paula told us all went well in the operating room. The doctor's asked her questions while the surgery was in progress and the staff had her writing something on a tablet. We believe he wanted to make sure he didn't cut into any important area around the tumor.

We were told the next step in treatment was that they were sending Paula to a rehab center in Oklahoma City for ten days followed by radiation. Dr. Sughrue had prescribed some meds that would be given at discharge. While in rehab, we made plans to have Paula stay with us until she could return to her home. We rearranged the living room so that a bed and furniture were configured to make the place private and homey. When we brought Paula home, we began looking at what diets were best to ward off cancer. During her first week, we went to our first appointment with her oncologist, Dr. Battiste, and Dr. Sughrue, the neurosurgeon in the Stephenson Cancer Center in Oklahoma City.

Dr. Sughrue explained the surgery to us and how he removed all the tumor in Paula's brain. While encouraging, he stated the tumor could come back and most patients didn't live past 15 months, which we didn't like to hear, but decided we were going to do all we could to fight this. When we left, Paula said to me that the results didn't sound too encouraging. I told her we were going to do all we could to fight it together. Dr. Battiste had made an appointment with the radiation oncologist in the Stephenson Center for the following week.

Durning our meeting with the radiation oncologist, we were told that they would be taking Paula to a room where they'd make a radiation head mask to fit over her head and face to protect her during the weeks of radiation treatments. After that, they showed us the pics of Paula's brain and where the radiation would be concentrated. I had asked the oncologist if they could use proton radiation rather than ionization radiation, which affects the surrounding area, but proton radiation does not, and is safer, in my opinion. He said he'd get with his staff and discuss the best radiation to use for Paula. As it turned out, they chose ionization.

A week later we met with one of Dr. Battiste's nurses who explained our options—there was a clinical trial and another option that Paula was interested in. A device called Optune, a cap-type device that fits to a patient's shaved head and delivers a continuous dose of low-intensity electric fields, improves survival and slows the growth of a deadly brain cancer along with chemotherapy.

At our next meeting, Dr. Battiste wanted to have Paula on the clinical trial first before the Optune cap. We were continuing the radiation. He had arranged for us to meet with the clinical trial clinicians and signed the paperwork before we left. Paula started the trial for a week with no side effects and Dr. Battiste reported all was good and we went to the lab for blood work after each visit. During the second week on the unknown agent, we got a call that I needed to take Paula to the OKC hospital immediately for platelet infusion. Her platelets were very low. We hopped into the car and raced up to the Health Sciences Center for the platelet infusion. After that, Paula was taken off the clinical trial. We continued with her other meds and radiation and waited to get the word on the Optune device.

The next appointment with Dr. Battiste was with his assistant, since he was out of town. Again, I felt the lady doc wasn't sure of herself. Paula was doing well at this point. When the doctor looked over Paula's meds, she determined that the steroid dose could be reduced. I felt Paula was doing so well, why change it without Dr. Battiste's approval? Two days later in the morning while Paula was resting in her bed, I had a hard time getting her to respond to my questions. She was coming in and out of unconsciousness. Minutes later, I stood over her calling out her name.

No response.

My heart raced. I could see the fear in Charmaine's eyes when I called 911. The EMT personnel came with strobe lights flashing and sirens blasting. I immediately told them her history and that she was Dr. Sughrue's patient at the OU Health Sciences Center. That Paula had been put on a reduced dosage of steroid and this happened. They began working with her and hurriedly rushed her out to the ambulance and continued working on her. At one point, the one EMT personnel said they were having a difficult time reviving her.

Charmaine and I sank in our overstuffed chairs, locked eyes, hearts pounding, and I said, "We can't lose her, Char."

The EMT personnel came in and said they were able to revive her and are rushing her up to the University hospital. I re-emphasized to the tech that they had to tell the nurse that Paula was Dr. Sughrue's patient, and his team should be contacted.

Charmaine and I hopped into our car and raced up to Oklahoma City. By the time we got there and parked and entered, Paula was in a bed in one of the ER rooms, unconscious. We looked around for someone to tell us what was going on.

Finally, a nurse came and said that Paula was going to be okay, but that it would take some time for her to recover from what they did to her.

The nurse was on Dr. Sughrue's team. We sat and prayed silently.

An hour later, the nurse returned and went to Paula, and we stood beside the bed close to her head. The nurse called out her name. Paula moved her head and opened her eyes.

She asked, "Do you know who this is?" pointing to Charmaine.

Paula said, "That's my mother."

"And who is that over there?"

"That's my dad."

"Good," said the nurse, giving us a thumbs up.

"She'll be groggy for a while," the nurse said. "She'll be able to go home today."

"Thank God!" I said.

A few days later, Paula and I went up to the Stephenson Center to see Dr. Battiste. I was wondering what he was going to say about the error his assistant made. He only mentioned it briefly and half-heartedly tried to apologize. I told him it was really a scary time for us. Paula just sat in her chair and listened. Such comments are expected from docs. They watch their words, so they won't be sued. That wasn't our intention, but we wanted it known how much we had feared for our daughter's life.

More blood work and Paula was approved for the Optune cap. By the time the device arrived, Paula went back into her apartment after spending a couple of months with us. She had her head shaved before we had the visit with a young lady with the Optune company in our home. She showed us how to fit the cap and arrange the cords that connected to the battery that hung in a container that would rest on Paula's hip. We were taught how to use the device and charged the batteries.

Paula was approved to drive again and was able to go on errands. She had retired from her position at the Norman YMCA because she felt she couldn't handle the pressure but was able to live alone in her apartment. We continued going to the Stephenson Center for radiation treatments and visiting with the radiation oncologist. In addition, we went for MRI scans before our visits with Dr. Battiste, who went over them with us to determine if any new tumors had appeared.

CHAPTER 45

Paula Marie's Second Surgery

The day Paula finished her radiation treatments, her aunt Jeanie and uncle Tony Ortiz were with us. We took pictures of her ringing the bell with the radiation techs who treated her, then she rang it alone. Finally, her aunt and uncle and I stood with her as she rang the bell. So far, she was doing well and getting around with her walker. She looked great.

Paula felt she couldn't maintain her apartment any longer and felt best if she went into an assisted living facility. After six months in Rivermont in Norman, we learned that a small tumor had appeared in the MRI scan. Dr. Battiste suggested we watch it for a while. Paula stopped the Optune. A few months passed and another MRI. Dr. Battiste decided she'd need to have another surgery.

And we thought our prayers were being answered. The fear and worry over our first-born were our constant companions. Now for both of us our burden became heavier.

This neurosurgeon was no Dr. Sughrue. He only met briefly with us before the surgery. He didn't have his patient awake during surgery like Dr. Sughrue. His bedside manner was lacking and after the surgery he didn't meet with us and Dr. Battiste. Pathetically, we never learned the outcome from him but only from Dr. Battiste.

As a side remark—it has been my experience that many surgeons are arrogant and lacking in bedside manner. They rarely see patients outside of the surgery suite, except for a visit before and after surgery.

They are not like most primary care physicians, who know their patient's history and try to get to know their patients.

In the waiting room were Charmaine and I, Leslie, our daughter, David Blanton, Paula's son, and wife, Megan, and Chuck and Gail Pendley. After the surgery, the neurosurgeon (I don't remember his name, what does that tell you?) came to the waiting room with another surgeon. They called out a family name and I was curious why our doctor was with him, and he didn't call out Paula's name. They looked at us—we were seated near the door—and we stood up and the other surgeon began telling us how well the surgery went with the patient. We were confused because he was talking about someone else and not our daughter. Then they left.

What was going on?

Megan Blanton, Paula's daughter-in-law, a nurse in Children's hospital and our daughter, Leslie, rushed out into the hall and cornered our neurosurgeon and his colleague and wanted to know what was going on and how did Paula's surgery go? Our neurosurgeon apologized. They realized what had happened and were talking in the hall about returning to talk to us, when Megan confronted them. He said all went well, but that was the last we saw of him. If I were chief of staff, he'd be gone out the front door.

Paula was transported to the Rehab center after a few days, the one she went to after her first surgery. After a week, we moved her to an assisted living facility in Norman, which was a poor one. Their service was subpar, and they didn't give her as much physical therapy as needed. I never saw the doctor that went through the facility, but Paula said she did visit her.

We moved her out after ten days to Brookhaven, an excellent facility. The medical officer, Dr. Paul Plusquellec, was excellent and had a great bedside manner. The staff worked well with Paula.

Several months later, it was decided to move Paula to Grace Assisted Living Center, where our primary care doctor was the medical officer. She had a nice room she shared with another lady. Her room had a TV, small fridge, large bathroom and a bed next to the window. She found it comfortable and acceptable.

CHAPTER 46
March 2020: Covid-19 Outbreak in the World

March 12, 2020, brought an epidemic in our nation. A corona virus, labeled Covid-19, escaped from a Chinese research lab in 2019, known as the Wuhan Lab; and hence, the virus was called the Wuhan virus by many. Covid-19 became a pandemic in the world. In response to the Covid-19 pandemic in the U.S., a series of lockdowns to mitigate the spread of the virus were introduced in March 2020. Schools and churches were closed, as well as some businesses. Everyone was required to wear a face mask, and all businesses and supermarkets had hand sanitation stands with rolled paper towels to wipe off carts and one's hands. Everywhere you looked, people had half of their faces covered. Difficult to recognize the ones you knew.

In Covid -19, "CO" stands for 'corona', 'Vi' for virus, and 'D' for the disease. Formerly known as "2019 novel coronavirus or "2019-nCoV."

Grace Center was in lockdown, and we were compelled to wear Hazmat suits before we went into the facility. It was cumbersome, but necessary according to the head nurse at Grace. Only one of us was allowed in Paula's room at a time and for only 30 minutes, and never more than once a day. Charmaine and I were never allowed to visit with our daughter together, which didn't seem logical to us. We both could have worn the Hazmat suits. I talked to many of the families outside of the facility. They were heartbroken over the rule that they could visit with their loved ones for only thirty minutes. Before Covid, I stayed with Paula for a couple of hours talking, taking care of her needs, and watching TV with her.

One elderly lady in a wheelchair in the hall outside Paula's room was telling the nurse and I that she must have been the worst mother in the world because none or her children came to visit her. The nurse said, "Honey. There is a virus going around and we are in lockdown."

I don't believe she understood. I felt so sorry for her. I tried to talk to her to make her feel better, but she seemed to be in the frame of mind that she failed her children.

Paula got Covid but her body fought it and after two negative testings she was free from the virus. Her sisters became creative and visited with Paula outside her window. We brought chairs and stayed long enough to have a good visit. There was a time when the weather was nice, we opened the window from outside and talked with her. This went on for about four months.

In late June, our primary care physician informed me that Paula wasn't doing well, she was dehydrated, her vitals were not good, and that we should think about putting her in hospice. That floored me.

Not yet, I thought. *Lord, not yet.*

I told him that the family wanted her treated as long as possible. So, he complied. A couple weeks passed, and her body was not responding to treatment. I talked with her nurse practioner, and she suggested we should really think about putting Paula in hospice to make her comfortable. I talked with our doctor, and he said her body was struggling, and it would be best. We decided to put her in hospice only if Paula agreed. The hospice nurse came with me to discuss it with Paula. I could tell she was sad, and I saw a tear flowing down her face, which tore me up inside.

My daughter facing death. How can this be happening?

We told her any time she wanted out, she had the right. She nodded. Two weeks later, I got a call from the hospice tech that she only had a couple of days. I visited with her one more time and the day before she died, Paula's sister Cindy spent time with her. She was heavily sedated but was able to wave and smile.

That evening, I got a call that Paula would probably only make it to noon the next day, July 9th. I told the nurse I would get up early and get there. I wanted to be with her before she passed. I got up and called and she was still with us. I got there around eight and by the time I put on the Hazmat suit and went to her room she had passed. The nurse's aides met me at the door and said it would be a few more minutes, that they were preparing her body.

I felt emotionless and in a trance sitting in the hall outside her room. Tears flowed down my cheeks. I wanted so to be with her for her last few minutes before she went home to be with the Lord. Once I went in, they had her body covered with a white sheet, but her face was exposed. I sat next to her and laid my face on hers and kissed her and told her I loved her and would be seeing her in heaven. I helped her fight the cancer for three years and because of Covid I couldn't be with my daughter when she passed. If I didn't have to put on the Hazmat, I could have made it to hold her hand and talk to her.

Another one of our children gone.

I thought about the time when she was born in Jackson, Mississippi, and how she grew up to be such a sweet and loving person. Why did this have to happen to her? Their mother and I loved our children and wanted to see them happy and secure before we left this earth.

When I got home, Charmaine and I embraced and had our cry. She said, "It hurts losing one, but losing two is more than a person can handle."

CHAPTER 47
In Remembrance of Our Oldest Daughter: Paula Marie

Havenbrook Funeral Home came to get Paula from Grace Living Center that morning around eleven o'clock, and the next day we went to their facility to make Paula's arrangements. The Magarian family, along with her son David Blanton, and daughter-in-law Megan, and Owen, her grandson, stricken with grief and trauma, sat in a large conference room looking at each other's sad faces. The attendant reviewed all the paperwork with us, ordered the death certificates, and filed Paula's obituary, which I wrote, so Havenbrook could place it in The Norman Transcript.

I could hear the attendant talking but I felt like I was at the end of a tunnel. We were told because of Covid, gatherings would be limited. The family would have their time one evening with Paula and the guest would visit the following evening without family present. That hit me like a ton of bricks. This was unacceptable to me, but we were forced to comply with the new Covid regulations. I so wanted to be present to greet all of Paula's friends and those of our family. The virus had everyone scared and most everyone stayed sheltered.

When the attendant finished with us, it was time to select the casket for Paula. I walked around like a zombie but tried not to show it. I never thought we'd ever see two of our children in caskets. It was agreed that an OU casket would be appropriate because Paula loved

OU football and was such a loyal fan.

Our family had our evening alone with Paula. Couldn't help but feel we failed her by not having her friends with us. The next evening, there surprisingly were a few dozen friends, who braved the Covid and visited Paula. We read their names in the book and thanked God for their kindness.

Three days later, the service was held in the Havenbrook chapel. Since Covid had turned everyone's world upside down, nothing was the same. So many dos and don'ts were in place, established by the government and the CDC. Paula had so many friends that if Covid wasn't a threat to life, the place would be packed, with standing room only.

Besides the family, there were about a dozen very close friends of Paula that attended regardless of Covid. Bishop Wallis Ohl celebrated Paula's life. Our granddaughter, Natalie, read a very emotional tribute that brought more tears, and she had a difficult time reading, made me wondered if she was going to be able to finish. Terri Angier, a dear friend of Paula's and our family, read an emotional message, too, that brought a flow of tears to everyone as she read her tribute.

We were so affected by Covid that nothing seemed right. I didn't write a tribute to her like I did Bob, not because I loved him more, it had to do with the unusual environment that affected us in a way that we were not in our usual mindset.

When the service was over, the Havenbrook attendant opened Paula's casket and directed nonfamily members past the casket to say their goodbyes. Then she led the first and second rows of our family to say their goodbyes, Charmaine and I were last. As we stood by our Paula, Charmaine holding tightly to my arm, we felt dazed and heartbroken. We had done this before.

Our oldest daughter, now gone to Heaven.

We bent over the edge of the casket to give her one last kiss. While we stood a little longer, I was thinking about the time when she first said 'Dadda.'

How can it be that we have lost two of our children? Who can tell us why? Was it something we did?

We walked away in a trance, to be ushered to the limousine parked behind the hearse and dozens of cars behind the limousine. The pall bearers placed Paula's casket in the hearse. Everyone followed in a convoy to the IOOF Cemetery. The police officer who led the convoy to the cemetery parked his vehicle with the strobes flashing, in the middle of the street at the entrance. He got out and stood behind his car and placed his hand over his heart, standing at attention. That warmed my heart, and I waved a hand of blessings to him. He smiled.

The limousine driver pulled up next to the only grave with a canopy. Bishop Ohl, dressed in his white vestments, had left his car and was standing at the bars, waiting for the pall bearers to bring Paula. The family was ushered to the row of chairs next to the casket. Friends wearing masks were standing in the area behind the family, keeping six feet apart as was the rule during Covid.

I didn't hear a word Bishop Ohl had said. My mind concentrated on the casket. When he finished, he didn't walk in front of the family shaking their hands as normally done. It was as if everyone was afraid of touching one another. No hugging or kissing, as goes on after a service. I had been given a red rose and at the end of the service, I placed it on Paula's casket, bent over and kissed her casket. (Tears flow from my eyes as I write this.) Everyone went to their cars in a solemn state and said very little, only nodding to one another.

Our out- of-state families were unable to travel during the Covid restrictions because it was frowned upon to be in crowds. So, Charmaine and I were alone again with our thoughts for the next few weeks through prayer and trying to rationalize what had happened to us. We prayed and gave all our feelings to the Lord. We read through the many cards sent to us from Paula's friends and relatives, which lifted our spirits. I have chosen one to share with you, which was written by one of Paula's great friends to us. In her card she wrote:

Memories of Paula: A friend to all in high school—all races, ages, classes, males or females. When I moved to Norman, she introduced me to everyone she knew. We walked together to school, and I thought this girl knows everyone so quickly. She was very kind to her grandfather who was living with you all at the time. She had a sweet giggle just like her mom's giggle. She tended to roll her eyes when her dad made

a joke, instead of a giggle. She was so cute and tiny with beautiful light eyes that sparkled and danced. Paula was an encourager and loved by all who had the pleasure of meeting her.
Love and Prayers,
Cheryl Robinson Bumpus.

I prayed several times for a sign that Bob and Paula were okay in Heaven. A couple of weeks passed. No sign. Then on this Tuesday morning, I was in the kitchen organizing our vitamins and supplements we took every morning after breakfast. Before I left to go on a couple of errands. I had given Charmaine hers and I was taking mine. Being in a hurry, I had taken all but four capsules that were on the counter next to the water glass. I thought I'd wait and take 'em when I came back.

Two hours later I returned, carrying in groceries and placing the bags on another counter. I had forgotten about the four capsules that were on the counter next to the fridge. After finishing with the groceries, I happened to pass the other counter and glanced at the four capsules. Instead of lying next to the glass in no special order when I left, the capsules were now arranged in the shape of a cross—two capsules' ends were touching each other horizontally and two were touching vertically in the center of the horizontal capsules. I was stunned at their perfect arrangement into the shape of a cross.

I asked Charmaine if she had wheeled herself into the kitchen while I was gone. She said she hadn't and that she was reading the whole time I was gone. I asked her to come into the kitchen She wheeled herself in and wanted to know what was going on. I asked her to look at the counter and tell me what she saw.

She stared at the figure for a few minutes without saying a word.

"What do you see?" I asked, impatiently.

She said, "The capsules are in the shape of a cross."

I said, "Yes. I see it, too."

Then I told her what I had done. She knew I had prayed for a sign. We both became silent as we realized my prayers were answered.

I said, "Thank You, Lord. We got our sign that Bob and Paula are okay in Heaven."

Did God send and angel to arrange the capsules?

During the 2020 Covid pandemic, we gave serious thought about having our 34th Annual Norman Christmas Day Community Dinner, held at the Norman High School, but after discussing the situation with my staff, I decided it still wasn't safe and cancelled the event. I didn't want to be accused of spreading the virus, that is, if anyone came. That was the question. Would anyone come if we tried to arrange a safe environment? We figured no one would come.

Consequently, Christmas 2020 at the Magarian home was unlike any other in the past 34 years, during which time we never celebrated our family Christmas until the evening of the Christmas Day Dinner. It was strange to be home and not working at the Norman High School. Charmaine and I felt sad for the shut-ins we delivered meals to. Normally, our eight drivers would deliver some three hundred meals for Meals on Wheels and those who called my home to get on the list. We wondered how they were going to get their meals this Christmas. We prayed that some neighbor or relative would leave a meal at their door. No one entered the homes. Everything was left at the door during the first year of the pandemic.

Paula receiving her
BA degree in Accounting

Paula with her dearest friends

CHAPTER 48

In Remembrance of My Brother: Dr. Edward O. Magarian

Earlier I wrote about my brother Ed, who was at Ole Miss with Charmaine and me, lived with us in Jackson, Mississippi when Paula was born, and was with us for a short time when he studied for his Ph.D. with me, both under the same professor, Dr. Lewis Nobles back at Ole Miss. Even though he was five years younger than I, we became very close and grew to love one another.

On Sunday December 06, 2020, Ed's son Kevin met him and his mother, Sandy, at Hardee's in West Fargo for breakfast. Kevin sat across from his dad and noticed his color was off. He thought it was the sun peeping through the blinds. When he moved in to look closer, he realized Ed had a yellowish tint to his skin.

Kevin told his dad, "You're jaundiced,"

Ed responded. "No, I'm not."

Kevin insisted and Ed said he'd see his primary care doc on Monday to get checked. Kevin wouldn't have it and said, "No! You're going to the emergency room today!"

Kevin drove his dad and mom to the ER and checked him in. The nurses lead them to one of the examining rooms and had Ed put on a gown. When he took off his shirt, they noticed how yellow his chest was. The doctor ordered a CT scan. After they brought Ed back to the examining room, the doctor came in and told them Ed had a tumor on the edge of his pancreas.

That evening, Ed was taken into surgery where a stint was inserted into his common bile duct to allow drainage. Ed's color started to improve the next day. It was then confirmed that Ed had pancreatic cancer.

Kevin reached out to his contacts at the Mayo Clinic, who put him in contact with the Director of the Cancer Institute. In two days, the director lined up a series of appointments for Ed and they headed to Mayo in Rochester. Ed was scheduled to see their best doctors in Pancreatic Cancer, GI Cancer surgery, and Pulmonary surgery. After visiting with the trifecta of doctors, they scheduled Ed for three surgeries: one to insert a chemo port, another to biopsy his liver, and the third was to remove an area of his right lung where there was a small mass that tested positive.

Ed's original prognosis was two to three months. He underwent chemotherapy and made it past two years from the time he was diagnosed with pancreatic cancer.

He passed into eternity on November 06, 2021

Ed & Sandy Magarian's family

CHAPTER 49
Life Goes On, But Memories Remain

Just as you think the pain is fading away, it returns. Then the lonely days can start over if you let it, but Jesus said, "Blessed are those who morn, for they will be comforted."

Charmaine and I learned that prayer and trust in God are essential when facing misfortunes in life. Staying connected and seeking His guidance, strength, and comfort through prayer provided solace and perspective during our difficult times. A form of worship for us was sitting in silence and listening for His still small voice. We believe that when we seek His presence, He hears our prayers, and orders our steps, and over time puts peace back into our hearts.

I tried writing again during the years of our losses to keep my mind active and free, but I didn't feel creative for a couple of months after the loss of Bob and Paula. I realized I had to force myself to get my creative juices flowing again from my writing. It helped me cope by getting that part of my life back.

In early fall of 2020, few months after Paula died, I began working on my second detective thriller, *The Tongue Collector*, introducing again my two favorite detectives, Noel McGraw and Holly Roark. I worked with my co-author, detective Scott Waldrup, for over a year, and we published in November 2021, at which time I presented a talk and a book signing at the west end Pioneer Library under the supervision of Nelson Dent. In previous talks I usually had close to

25 people in attendance, but at this event only eight people showed up and many were friends of our granddaughter, Natalie Stephens. Covid still had a hold on people, and they feared crowds, but, for me, 2021 was post Covid and I no longer felt the need to wear a mask, or stop giving talks, or stop going places. After having all the vaccine and boosters, I wasn't going to let Covid stop me.

My third detective thriller, *Forever Young*, plotted and written with my co-author, detective (ret.) Mike Issac was moving along in early 2022, and we published in 2023. I have yet to give a talk or book signing on this latest detective novel at the library because of a change in policy, and the lack of publicity; no one signed up for my presentation. In previous years Nelson Dent did a fabulous job in stirring up interest in my work.

While I am writing and still love to write, I must divide my time between writing and taking care of Charmaine. Her health is good, but her knees are bad, and we've decided not to have the surgery. Consequently, she navigates in a wheelchair. I'm here for her, and help her, and haven't forgotten all she did for me in all our years together.

I'm reminded of the time when we were at the eye institute in Oklahoma City for an appointment. After seeing our ophthalmologist, Char had to go to the restroom. There were no special family units that I could take her into. We found an isolated area with separate restrooms for women and men. I wheeled her into the women's and took her to the handicap stall against the wall. While she was engaged, two women entered and went into the adjacent stalls. Char was done, but I waited until I heard them leave their stalls and move to the wash basins. I wheeled Char out to one of the basins while the ladies were drying their hands on paper towels.

I said, "Sorry ladies, I hope you don't mind me being in here, but we couldn't find any other place." They smiled and said, as they dried their hands, "No, that's fine." One of the ladies rushed over with paper towels as I was washing Char's hands. I noticed tears in her eyes as she smiled at me. I thanked her, believing she was emotionally moved that I was taking care of the love of my life.

Once this memoir is published, I plan on writing another nonfiction work about my father who practiced medicine for over fifty years. I have selected the working title: *My Father, The Doctor*. I assisted my dad intermittently for four years while in high school. The practice of medicine was different back in the '40s. Docs were general practitioners, having the title of *Physician and Surgeon*. My dad made house calls and had evening hours. The doctors had very little to assist them in their diagnoses, only X-ray, blood work, and urinalyses. We witnessed the development of penicillin during WWII. The doctors then had to be great diagnosticians, and my dad was the best. He had to be, since there were no CT scans, MRIs, PET scans, computers, or cell phones.

He taught me a couple of good lessons in the practice of medicine: "Listen to your patients, they will tell you much that will help in your diagnoses," and "Show compassion for your patients, it's part of the healing process."

It is my wish to contrast the doctors back then with those of today, who base many of their diagnoses on all the programed technology before they touch a patient—that is, if they ever get away from their computers.

The End

ACKNOWLEDGMENTS

Writing is a lonely task which I find enjoyable. Having a team that brings life to my books is rewarding. I wish to thank those who have contributed to *Amazing Love, It Can Be, A Memoir.*

My life's partner, Charmaine Magarian, for her input into our book. Thanks for helping me remember some details of our life together.

Dr. Dewey D. Garner, my Ole Miss friend, for his suggestions and reliving some of the "good ole days" at Ole Miss.

H. Gary Apoian, attorney and author, for his interest in this work.

Editor: Nancy Hancock, the consummate language scholar and eagle-eyed corrector and best editor and advisor a writer can have.

Best Cover Designer: Peter O'Connor in the UK. He can be reached at www.bespokebookcovers.com.

Best Formatting and Publication: Amy Atwell, Author E.M.S.

My family: Thanks for your love and support. Love you all.

Robert Magarian, B.A., BSPh, Ph.D., is professor emeritus of medicinal chemistry and pharmaceutics. He has been writing fiction since his retirement and has created several fictional characters in medical and detective thrillers. The two most popular characters are Detectives Cowboy Noah McGraw and Holly Roark of the Atlanta PD.

Magarian is the author of five thriller novels, *The Watchman*, *Seventy-Two Hours*, *You'll Never See Me Again*, *A Crime to Remember*, *The Tongue Collector*, and *Forever Young*.

In addition to his fiction, Magarian is the author of his latest nonfiction book: Amazing Love, It Can Be, a Memoir. He has also written two essays: *Follow Your Dream*, and *A Journey into Faith*. He lives with his family in Norman, Oklahoma.

www.ingramcontent.com/pod-product-compliance
Lightning Source LLC
Chambersburg PA
CBHW020440130626
46549CB00001B/226